Salisbury Vineyards'
Schoolhouse in Avila Valley

Wine In Everyday Cooking

Wine In Everyday Cooking

"Cooking With Wine for Family and Friends"

by Patricia Ballard

Edited by Pamela Kittler

Published by

THE WINE APPRECIATION GUILD

San Francisco

Other books published by The Wine Appreciation Guild:

THE CHAMPAGNE COOKBOOK
EPICUREAN RECIPES OF CALIFORNIA WINEMAKERS
GOURMET WINE COOKING THE EASY WAY
FAVORITE RECIPES OF CALIFORNIA WINEMAKERS
DINNER MENUS WITH WINE
EASY RECIPES OF CALIFORNIA WINEMAKERS
THE POCKET ENCYCLOPEDIA OF CALIFORNIA WINE
IN CELEBRATION OF WINE AND LIFE
WINE CELLAR RECORD BOOK
CORKSCREWS: Keys to Hidden Pleasures
THE CALIFORNIA WINE DRINK BOOK
THE CALIFORNIA BRANDY DRINK BOOK
NEW ADVENTURES IN WINE COOKERY
WINE IN EVERYDAY COOKING

THE VINTAGE IMAGE SERIES:

THE NAPA VALLEY TOUR BOOK
THE NAPA VALLEY WINE BOOK
THE SONOMA MENDOCINO TOUR BOOK
THE SONOMA MENDOCINO WINE BOOK
THE CENTRAL COAST TOUR BOOK
THE CENTRAL COAST WINE BOOK

Published by:

The Wine Appreciation Guild
360 Swift Avenue
S. San Francisco, CA 94080
(800) 231-9463
Info At: www.wineappreciation.com

Library of Congress Catalog Number: 82-062682
ISBN 0-932664-84-9
Printed in The United States of America
Designed by: Colonna, Caldewey, Farrell; Designers
Cover Photo: Bill Miller
Illustrations: Maury Tieman
Editor: Pamela Goyan Kittler

Table of Contents

DEDICATION

To: Van who always knew I would
and Bill who never thought I could.

Introduction

The purpose of this book is to teach you about good food made even better by the addition of little *good* wine, and to pass along the wisdom of my Grandmother. I'm sure she did not know the word "gourmet", but she did know that it wasn't necessary to purchase expensive or specialty foods to make a dish fit for any connoisseur. She was a firm believer in economy of time and movement. She taught me it is unnecessary to be a slave to either family or guest. She taught me to think about what I wanted to create (she always created!) before I went to the kitchen. She scoffed at what she called my concoctions and then, lovingly, pointed out my mistakes. She taught me that simple food was most often more delightful to the palate than complicated dishes that confused the taste buds. Her only law was to pay attention to the blending of flavors and colors. She believed food had to attract the smell and sight before it could ever please the palate, and she lived her convictions. One of my first and nicest memories is of my Grandmother's kitchen and the glorious smells one always found there. The big copper stock pot, gently simmering all the goodness it was possible to coax from bones and a few vegetables. The deep, rich golden loaves of bread that filled every room of the house with such smells that one's mouth watered with expectation. The bright red Marinara sauce that foretold pasta for dinner. No matter what time of day, there was food in one stage or another being prepared. No one ever left her home without, as she would say, "a little bite of something."

Smell was not the only sense stimulated in that kitchen. Wherever the eye focused, there was color. Pots of every imaginable kind of herb adorned the window sills. Baskets of red and green peppers, strings of sausages and garlic hanging on the walls; and in the pantry, a tiny little room off the kitchen, rows and rows of home canned fruits and vegetables. No decorator in the world ever created a more beautiful array of color than those rows of jars filled with pickled peaches, plum butter, spiced apricots and pears. Jars of pickled cucumbers spiked with snow-white cauliflower, devil red peppers and bright orange carrots, kept company with jars of golden corn and black-green aritchokes. Home-canned tomatoes, tomato sauce and the most glorious home-made catsup (never to be confused with those poor imitations to be found in stores) added yet more color. As a finale, there were the daintly little jars of raspberry, strawberry and blackberry jams that tasted like a summer afternoon and back in the kitchen, Grandma's copper pots and pans casting a rich warm glow in the late afternoon sunlight.

There was a sense of order and comfort in my Grandmother's kitchen that I have never experienced in any other. In that kitchen, I was privileged to listen, and as I grew a little older, participate in discussions ranging from politics and religion to history and philosophy. Quiet work, such as shelling fresh green peas, was the time for sharing secrets and dreams or confessing little sins and big disappointments. Above all, my Grandmother believed that food meant the coming together of family and friends. Meals were a time of conversation, of relaxing after a day of hard work. These are lessons I learned well, and they have kept me in good stead all my life.

For the cooks of today, who must often be housekeeper, spouse, parent and employee at the same time, it is more important than ever to remember the value of the coming together of family and friends for at least the evening meal. I know this is an idealistic approach in our changing culture, but it is a goal well worth working toward. We have a whole generation of young people who have grown up eating meals on the run or in front of television sets. They do not know how to have a conversation at the dining table, simply because most of them don't sit at the table! It is difficult to be gracious as an adult if one hasn't been taught to be gracious as a child. Today's cooks, unlike my Grandmother, have an incredible number of aids, varying from crockpots to microwave ovens, to help in the preparation of meals that bring people together. I sincerely hope, and firmly believe that every recipe in this book will also be a help: easy and quick for the most part and, as Grandma would say, "not just something to fill up a hollow spot in your stomach".

It would be ideal if everyone could use the wines I specify in this book, but I know that isn't possible. Therefore, I have tried to give you some good sub-stitutions. Since generic wines vary so greatly in taste, I usually suggest using varietal wines in the recipes. This is not to say that I never cook with generic wines -- I do, but only those generic wines I know well and like. It is important to know if a wine called Chablis is sweet or dry. It could make all the difference in the outcome of a dish. Marinating fresh fruit with a sweet Chablis is fine, but

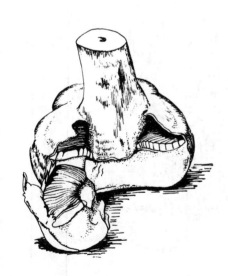

that same wine would destroy the delicate flavor of fish. Also certain varietal wines such as Barbera, Pinot Blanc, Pinot Noir and Chardonnay have such a distinctive taste that I feel that it is worth your while to check with more than one source before using a substitute, generic or otherwise. Remember you *cannot* cook with a wine you do not like well enough to drink. The alcohol burns off, leaving the flavor, which is why you are using wine. There really is no such thing as "cooking wine". This idea comes from the European custom hundreds of years ago of taking the very same wine that was drunk at the table and salting it so the cooks would not drink it. The so-called cooking wines of today are not drinkable and will ruin good food. I feel particularly strongly about this when it comes to Sherries and Vermouth. That 98¢ bottle of "Cooking Sherry" will really do you in. It is never given any time to age or to develop any real taste and is thus reduced to a harsh bouquet and a somewhat bitter taste. You will rarely use as much as a cup of Sherry in any recipe. Keep in mind that Sherry is a wine that has been liberally laced with brandy or other spirits and is, therefore, a fortified wine with an alcohol content of 19 to 21% by volume. This high volume of alcohol allows Sherries to remain stable for many months. You, in turn, need not be in a great hurry to finish these wines. A fine Sherry always performs magic with food. A bad Sherry only makes you the cook, look bad.

Vermouth, sweet and dry is used for both aperitifs and dessert wines and is made by adding herbs and spices. From one vintner to another, Vermouth is as different as the winemaker's personality. Some like sage, others do not; some like rosemary and thyme, others do not, and so on. My personal feeling about Vermouth is that it is the most versatile of all wines, both for drinking and cooking. Alas, most Americans think Vermouth is useful only to wave, and very quickly at that, over a dry martini! Never forget that Vermouth for cooking is like having a liquid herb garden sitting right on your kitchen shelf.

This may be as good a place as any to state my views of the "hard stuff". Martinis have been known to ruin more good bottles of wine and fine meals than just about anything I can think of! The taste buds are so benumbed that it becomes impossible for them to detect the delicate flavors of good wine and food. I have discussed this with many fine chefs and all agree that those who drink hard liquor before the meal, eat little of what they are served. My judgement of hard liquor is not a moral one, it is rather a protection of the taste buds.

Now the time has come to welcome you and your family in sharing with me and my family our love of fine food and wine, and the wish you may always enjoy the everlasting bounties the good Lord has bestowed upon us all.

Patricia Ballard
March 1981

About the Illustrator

I met Maury Tieman through friends who knew I was looking for a special person to illustrate this book. I knew almost immediately that he was the one I was searching for: not only is he a wonderfully talented artist, Maury has the "right" feeling for food as a catalyst for the coming together of family and friends, to savor and share. His enthusiasm and dedication to his work has been boundless and I appreciate that as much as his talent.

About the Editor

Pamela Goyan Kittler is a wine and food writer with considerable background in The California Wine Industry. After obtaining a degree in art history, (Phi Beta Kappa) from the University of California, Berkely, Pamela taught French cooking and catering in Berkeley.

She has worked in recipe development and wine tasting at Mirassou Winery and her recipes have been published in newspapers and winery publications.

Ms. Kittler is currently a free-lance food writer and editor in Northern California and also professionally tests and evaluates recipes.

Antipasto

The word antipasto means literally "before the pasta", and in Italy it is quite simple. A few raw vegetables with a simple dip or cheese and crackers served with a good Dry Sherry, a Vermouth cocktail or any wine of your choice. It can be an elegant affair, as well as easy, when something like pate and champagne are served. But let us understand that antipasto is not the meal. It is, rather, a most civilized custom of relaxing and removing the raw edge of hunger before the meal. To me, the importance is the relaxation—putting aside the day in order to welcome the evening.

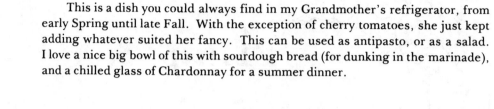

ANTIPASTO SALAD

This is a dish you could always find in my Grandmother's refrigerator, from early Spring until late Fall. With the exception of cherry tomatoes, she just kept adding whatever suited her fancy. This can be used as antipasto, or as a salad. I love a nice big bowl of this with sourdough bread (for dunking in the marinade), and a chilled glass of Chardonnay for a summer dinner.

Notes from Patti:

If tomatoes are left too long in marinade they tend to become soggy. The other vegetables only get better. You can add green beans, whole kernel corn, diced beets, almost anything you like. You can always cheat a little (I do sometimes) by using canned artichokes and onions that are packed in water.

Vegetables:

8 to 10 large cooked artichokes,
  cut in 8ths
12 to 14 small whole pearl
  onions, cooked
1 to 2 lbs. fresh mushrooms, cut
  in ¼ths
2 1 lb. cans pitted green olives
2 1 lb. cans pitted black olives
1 1 lb. can garbanzo beans
1 4 oz. jar pimentos
Cherry tomatoes

Dressing:

¾ cup olive oil
½ cup red wine vinegar
5 large cloves garlic, finely
  minced
1 heaping Tbsp. dry mustard
1 tsp. dill weed

Place all vegetables, except cherry tomatoes, in a large bowl.

Pour all dressing ingredients into food processor or blender and blend until thoroughly mixed. Pour dressing over vegetables and toss several times. Cover and refrigerate at least 8 hours before serving. Chill cherry tomatoes separately and add enough for each individual portion just before serving. Toss well. Serves 10.

PATTI'S PATÉ

I love to make people feel "special", whether it's in our tasting room, my home, or remembering them with something I have created just for them. So, just for you, something very special from me.

*½ lb. (2 cubes) butter (only
    butter will do)
1 lb. fresh chicken livers,
    trimmed of all fat
½ lb. fresh mushrooms, thinly
    sliced
1 large bunch green onions
    (use half of green tops and all
    of the white root sections),
    thinly sliced
4 to 6 medium cloves of garlic,
    thinly sliced
l tsp. salt
½ tsp. dried rosemary, crumbled
½ tsp. dill weed (I like more)
1 tsp. dry mustard
⅔ cup Chardonnay**

Melt one cube of butter in large skillet over low heat. Add mushrooms, onions and garlic. Sauté for 3 to 5 minutes, stirring constantly. Push vegetables to the sides of the skillet. Add chicken livers and cook only until edges turn white; turn at once. Add salt, rosemary, dill weed and mustard; stir thoroughly, add Chardonnay, stirring again and cook until liquid is reduced to half. Cut second cube of butter in ¼ths. Place butter in a blender or food processor fitted with a chopping blade and add remaining ingredients. Blend until smooth. If using a blender, alternate a small amount of cooked ingredients with a small amount of butter and blend. Continue until all ingredients are blended smoothly. Refrigerate and let flavors meld 24 hours before serving. Wonderful served on slices of french bread together with ice cold champagne as a first course. Serves 20 dieters or 10 non-dieters.

*A *dry* French Colombard may be substituted for the Chardonnay.

Notes from Patti:

I like to use old-fashioned pickling jars, the ones with glass tops and rubber rings, for this pate. They can be used as storage containers, are decorative as serving dishes, and make great gifts. The pate will keep up to 10 days in the refrigerator, and freezes well for as long as 3 months.

PIZZA WITH PIZZAZ

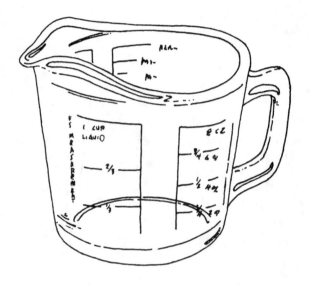

Dough:

*1 cake fresh yeast (or 1 pkg.
   dry yeast)*
2 Tbsps. lukewarm water
1 tsp. salt
3 Tbsps. butter
1 cup hot water
*3 cups all purpose flour, sifted
   twice*

Topping:

½ cup Parmesan cheese
*½ lb. Mozzarella cheese, cut in
   slices*
2 cups Marinara sauce (see page 59)
1 tsp. thyme

Notes from Patti:

This pizza is very good as is. However, the recipe is very basic and you may add any food your imagination allows. I won't make a pizza without anchovies unless I am using sea food such as shrimp or crab meat. If you use tomatoes, be sure they are fresh and not canned. Canned tomatoes contain too much juice and will make your pizza soggy.

Place lukewarm water in a small bowl and crumble or sprinkle the yeast over the top. Set aside. Place the salt and butter in a large mixing bowl and pour in the hot water. Cool to room temperature and add the dissolved yeast. Add half of the flour and beat until smooth. Add remaining flour and continue to beat until smooth and glassy. Turn dough into a large lightly oiled bowl and turn until dough is lightly oiled on all sides. Cover with a damp cloth and place in a warm place until dough has doubled in size -- about 45 minutes to 1 hour. Punch down and shape into desired size, making sure to form a thick edge. Place on lightly oiled pizza pan (or any other large, flat pan) or cookie sheet and brush liberally with olive oil.

Sprinkle ½ cup Parmesan cheese on top of dough. Add half of the Mozzarella slices. Add the Marinara sauce. Top with the remaining Mozzarella and sprinkle with thyme. Bake in a 450° oven until golden brown -- 15-20 minutes. Makes 1 large pizza.

SESAME CHEESE THINS

> *1 lb. sharp cheddar cheese,*
>   *grated*
> *½ lb. (2 cubes) butter*
> *2 Tbsps. Cream Sherry*
> *2 cups flour*
> *½ tsp. garlic salt*
> *1 cup sesame seeds*

Cream cheese, butter and Cream Sherry until fluffy. Add flour and garlic salt. Make into rolls one inch in diameter and six inches in length and wrap rolls in waxed paper. Refrigerate for two hours (or keep in freezer until needed). Cut into ⅓ inch slices, dip in sesame seeds. Bake at 400° for ten minutes. The unbaked dough will freeze for up to two months. Baked and kept in a tightly covered container, they will stay fresh about 10 days. Serves 15 to 20.

QUICK HORS D'OEUVRE MEATBALLS

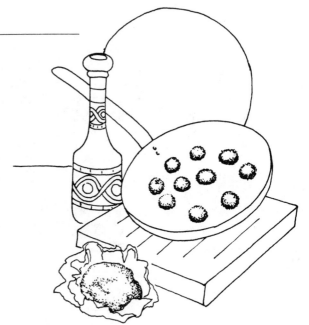

> *Meatballs:*
>
> *2 lbs. lean ground beef*
> *⅔ cup dry bread crumbs*
> *2 eggs*
> *4 Tbsps. steak sauce (Prime*
>   *Choice is good)*
> *2 Tbsps. vegetable oil*
>
> *Sauce:*
>
> *⅓ cup steak sauce*
> *⅓ cup Almond Marsala**
> *2 Tbsps. light brown sugar*
> *3 Tbsps. butter, melted*

Combine the first 4 ingredients of the meatballs. Shape into 1'' balls. Brown the meatballs in the oil in a large skillet. Drain fat from meatballs. Add the sauce to the meatballs and simmer, covered, 15 minutes.

Makes 75 meatballs the size of a walnut.

*Amaretto may be substituted for the Almond Marsala.

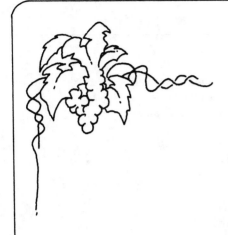

Salad

My dictionary describes salad as "green vegetables (lettuce, endive, romaine, etc.) often with tomato, cucumber or radish served with dressing". I find that to be a most inadequate definition. A salad can be anything from gelatin to rice. Salads can be as elaborate or simple as you wish -- anything from a great Caesar salad to a simple beet and onion ring mixture. It is certainly possible to have a different kind of salad every single day of the year if one chooses to do so. Salads, hot or cold, offer a rainbow of colors to the eye and a panoply of texture to the palate. So get out of the lettuce and tomato rut and into using your imagination!

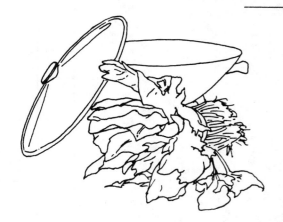

WILTED SPINACH SALAD

*2 bunches fresh spinach, washed
   and torn into bite size pieces*
*4 strips lean bacon, cut into bite
   size pieces*
*4 fresh green onions, including
   green tops, chopped*
½ cup red wine vinegar
2 heaping Tbsps. fine sugar
2 Tbsps. soysauce
1 tsp. dry mustard
1 hard boiled egg yolk, crumbled

Fry bacon in large pan; remove and set aside. Add onions to fat and wilt. Mix in wine vinegar, sugar, dry mustard and soy sauce. Add spinach and keep tossing until all the pieces are well coated. Serve on heated plates -- garnish with the bacon pieces and egg yolk. Serves 4.

CHILLED AND DILLED CUCUMBERS

Salad:

3 cucumbers
1 Tbsp. salt

Dressing:

¾ cup red wine vinegar
1 tsp. sugar
¼ tsp. white pepper
1 tsp. dill weed

Notes from Patti:

I use my electric Wok to prepare this dish at the table. The aroma is fantastic and guests can hardly wait to be served!!!

Scrub cucumbers free of waxy coating and dry them. Score the cucumbers with the tines of a fork. Slice as thinly as possible (the slices should be transparent). Place the slices in a deep bowl and sprinkle them with salt. Then cover them directly with a plate and weigh it down with something heavy, pressing the slices. Let them stand at room temperature for 2 hours. Drain the slices and press out any remaining liquid.

Combine the vinegar, sugar and pepper and pour over the cucumber slices. Chill these thoroughly and at serving time drain the slices and sprinkle them with dill. Serves 4.

MICHAEL'S FAVORITE SALAD

Even as a small child, my son Michael would choose raw vegetables over sweet snacks. While other mothers were trying to force vegetables on their children, Michael often made a meal of salad and sourdough bread. He has always been discriminating about food, without being finicky.

Salad:

1 large clove fresh garlic, peeled
1 cup spinach, shredded
1 cup cabbage, shredded
1 cup head lettuce, shredded
1 cup curly endive, shredded
5 anchovy fillets
3 Tbsps. Roquefort cheese,
  crumbled

Dressing:

½ tsp. paprika
¼ tsp. dry mustard
½ tsp. black pepper, freshly
  ground
2 Tbsps. red wine vinegar
6 Tbsps. olive oil
½ cup sour cream
1 Tbsp. instant onion, toasted
4 slices bacon, crisply cooked
  and crumbled

Rub wooden salad bowl with garlic and discard. Toss greens together in the bowl. Cut anchovies in small pieces and sprinkle over greens. Add crumbled Roquefort cheese.

Mix paprika, mustard, pepper and vinegar. Add oil, a little at a time, and beat thoroughly. Blend in sour cream.

Toss greens with the dressing until well coated. Garnish with crumbled bacon and toasted instant onion. Serves 6 to 8.

Notes from Patti:

The secret of any green salad is totally dry greens -- my hair blower is as important in my kitchen as in my bathroom -- use the "cool" setting to dry everything from greens to fresh fruit.

Head lettuce must be broken by hand -- never cut with a knife as this will bruise the lettuce.

Leaf lettuce may be broken by hand or cut with a knife. Always discard stalks.

Tips for washing spinach -- add one tablespoon baking soda to ½ gallon water. Rinse twice, the second rinse under cold running water. Soda helps the removal of sand and grit.

I never use plastic or metal containers for marinating anything. Plastics tend to retain all the flavors of past uses, and metals will add their own taste when exposed to the acidity of vinegar or lemon juice.

ITALIAN GREEN BEAN SALAD

Notes from Patti:

The Italian green bean, sometimes called the Romano bean, is slightly wider and flatter than the Kentucky Wonder. If you grow these beans you will find their color is almost identical to that of the leaves so that they are well camouflaged. The texture of the Italian bean is softer and more tender than that of other varieties.

This delicious, taste tantalizing salad demonstrates my theory of easy preparation with available products. Since this recipe takes only minutes to prepare, it can be done before you go to work. Any "do ahead" dish is a plus!

> 1 lb. fresh Italian green beans,
>   cooked and cut in thirds
> 1 medium-sized sweet red onion,
>   cut into rings
> ⅓ cup red wine vinegar
> 3 Tbsps. olive oil
> 2 large cloves garlic, crushed
> ½ tsp. dill weed
> Salt and freshly ground black
>   pepper to taste

Combine all ingredients and toss several times. Place in covered container and chill 8 hours. Remove garlic cloves before serving. This is best when served on a bed of curly endive lettuce. Serves 6.

BUTTERMILK DRESSING

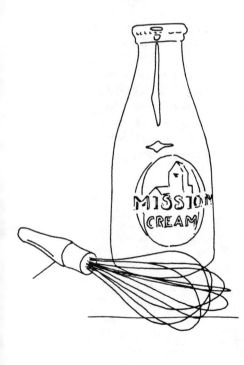

Really let your imagination take over with this recipe! Great for green salads, of course, but try it with fruit salad too. Serve it over well chilled chunks of fresh pineapple or dip fresh strawberries in it. Use it with fish for a marvelous change from tarar sauce. Use it for a different potato salad or a topping for baked potatoes.

> 3 cups mayonnaise
> 1 cup buttermilk
> 1 tsp. garlic powder
> 6 oz. bleu cheese
> 1 tsp. dill weed (optional)
> 1 Tbsp. parsley, finely minced
> Black pepper to taste, finely
>   ground

Place all ingredients in a blender or a food processor fitted with a chopping blade, and blend until smooth. Chill for several hours.

MAYONNAISE
(Blender or Food Processor Method)

There are many variations of homemade mayonnaise. This happens to be the one I like the best. I vary the taste with seasonings. For cold salmon add a teaspoon of dried dill weed. For fresh fruit salads or chilled slices of pineapple add a few grinds of nutmeg. Add several tablespoons of a very hot mustard to mayonnaise to serve with boiled beef.

> *2 egg yolks*
> *1 tsp salt*
> *2 Tbsps. white wine vinegar*
> *1½ tsps. sugar*
> *1 tsp. dry mustard*
> *½ tsp. white pepper*
> *1½ cups olive oil*

Add first six ingredients to blender or food processor fitted with a chopping blade and blend until smooth, 3 to 4 seconds. Continue processing, adding olive oil in a slow, steady stream. Pour into a canning jar and refrigerate until well chilled. This will keep easily ten days. Makes about 2 cups.

Notes from Patti:

Never try to double a homemade mayonnaise recipe. The doubling of oil will tend to make the mayonnaise separate.

GINGER SALAD DRESSING

This is great on cabbage and cucumbers. I also like to marinate small, whole mushrooms in this dressing.

> *3 Tbsps. red wine vinegar*
> *3 Tbsps. soy sauce*
> *1 Tbsp. fine sugar*
> *3 Tbsps. olive oil*
> *1 clove garlic, crushed*
> *1 tsp. ginger, freshly grated*

Place all ingredients in a blender or a food processor fitted with a chopping blade and blend for one minute.

Notes from Patti:

Fine sugar (or bar sugar) dissolves very easily, and is, therefore, good for uncooked dressings and sauces.

Soup

The art of making and serving good, rich homemade soup is almost unpracticed today. There is a whole generation of people who have never even eaten homemade soup: as far as they're concerned, all soup comes from a can. I am not against all canned soups; they can be useful in preparing a number of dishes. There is, however, really no comparison between homemade soup or stock and their canned counterparts. People complain that soup making takes too much time and effort. When you realize that 99% of the time involved is the cooking itself, the effort becomes worthwhile. There is nothing like the aroma of simmering soup to whet the appetite and bolster one's spirits.

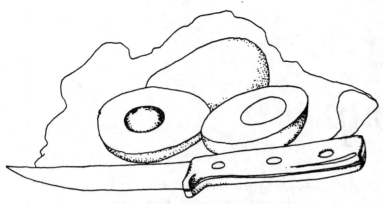

COLD AVOCADO SOUP

Soup:

*3 large very ripe avocadoes,
    peeled, pitted and cut in
    chunks*
1 cup chicken broth
1 cup half and half cream
4 Tbsps. lemon juice
4 Tbsps. Dry Sherry

Garnish:

4 paper thin slices of lemon

Place all soup ingredients in blender or food processor fitted with a chopping blade, and blend until smooth. Serve well chilled. Garnish each serving with a slice of lemon. Serves 4.

Notes from Patti:

Never try to ripen avocados on a window sill in direct light. The avocado does not ripen all the way to the pit. The best way to ripen the fruit is to bury them in your flour sack.

A great trick to keep an avocado dish, such as the cold soup, from turning an ugly brown color is drop one or two of the pits into the mixture and cover with plastic wrap. Works every time!

CANTALOUPE SOUP

Soup:

*1 large ripe cantaloupe, about
    2½ to 3 lbs.*
½ cup Dry Sherry
¼ cup sugar
1 Tbsp. lime juice

Garnish:

4 paper thin slices of lime

Cut cantaloupe in half and discard seeds. Scoop out meat and place in blender or food processor fitted with a chopping blade. Add remaining soup ingredients and blend until very smooth. Refrigerate, covered, until very cold. Serve in chilled soup bowls and float one lime slice on top. Serves 4.

SHERRY SPINACH SOUP

> 4 Tbsps. butter
> 3 Tbsps. flour
> 2 cups milk
> 1 cup light cream (or evaporated
>   milk)
> 1 cup spinach cooked, chopped
>   and well-drained
> 1 beef bouillon cube, dissolved
>   in ½ cup boiling water
> 3 Tbsps. Dry Sherry
> 1 small whole onion studded with
>   3 whole cloves
> Salt and white pepper, to taste

Place butter, flour, one cup of the milk, the cream and spinach in a blender or food processor fitted with a chopping blade. Blend until liquified. Pour mixture into a double boiler, heat thoroughly. Add bouillon liquid and rest of milk, stir until creamy. Add Dry Sherry, onion and salt and pepper to taste -- simmer 8 to 10 minutes. Chill 3 to 4 hours. Remove onion before serving. Serve cold. Serves 4.

SPLIT PEA SOUP

I like to serve this soup with a pot of sour cream on the table to let everyone add as much as they like. If a nice hamhock is available, add at the very beginning for a delicious variation.

> 2 cups dry split peas
> 8 cups water
> 1 cup Chenin Blanc*
> ½ bay leaf
> 1 medium potato, scrubbed and
>   diced
> 1 onion, coarsely diced
> 1 tsp. curry powder
> ¼ tsp. oregano
> 1 tsp. smoked salt

Bring water to a rolling boil and add peas and salt. Boil 15 minutes, add remaining ingredients. Cover and simmer about 1½ hours. Serves 6.
*A Rhine style wine may be substituted for the Chenin Blanc.

Notes from Patti:

There is no subtitute for Dry Sherry. You *must* use a good Sherry. The 98¢ cooking Sherry is the worst possible choice and will spoil any recipe. The three types of Sherry are: Dry (sometimes called Pale Dry) -- with a lovely nutty taste; Medium Dry or Cocktail Sherry; and Sweet (sometimes called Cream) -- used mostly for desserts. All Sherrys are fortified (laced with Brandy) and will last a very long time after opening.

SONNY PETERSON'S MINESTRONE SOUP

My friend, Sonny Peterson, is a whirlwind of energy and activity: mother of two almost teenagers, wife of Fire Dept. Captain Wayne Peterson and Girl Scout leader for the last ten years. The Petersons live on a small farm in the Soquel mountains and Sonny takes advantage of the space by growing a great deal of their food. She also cans and freezes excess fruits and vegetables for future use. Sonny says the secret to her minestrone is the garden fresh vegetables she uses.

This soup isn't just good -- it's great!

Soup:

8 cups beef stock
¼ cup parsley, chopped
⅛ tsp. rosemary
1 cup onions, coarsely minced
2 Tbsps. olive oil
1 16 oz. can kidney beans,
    drained and rinsed
1 cup Swiss chard, finely chopped
½ cup lima beans
½ cup fresh string beans, cut in thirds
1 cup broccoli flowerettes
1 cup potatoes, diced
1 cup celery, finely sliced
3 cups cabbage, shredded
1 cup Semolina noodles (macaroni or flat)
1 32 oz. can V-8 juice
½ cup barley, precooked
1 cup leftover roast beef or steak,
    diced
½ cup Dry Sherry

Garnish:

3 large cloves garlic, finely minced
3 Tbsps. parsley, finely minced
Parmesan cheese, freshly grated

Simmer stock with parsley and rosemary for 20 minutes. Strain and return to pot. Sauté onions in a separate pan in olive oil for 5 minutes. Add to reheated stock with beans, vegetables and noodles. Bring to a boil and cook until vegetables are almost tender, about 10 minutes. Then add V-8 juice, barley, meat and Dry Sherry. Reheat. Just before serving sprinkle each bowl with garlic and parsley. Pass the Parmesan cheese.

This soup freezes beautifully; just omit noodles and add them when reheating. Serves 6 generously.

MAMA'S QUICK ONION SOUP

This can be prepared in a single large casserole, but the individual casseroles are much more festive. You may substitute three cans of beef broth, but Mama wouldn't like it, and neither would I!

6 large onions, coarsely diced
1 Tbsp. olive oil
2 Tbsps. butter
6 cups beef stock
6 Tbsps. Dry Sherry
6 slices sourdough bread,
* toasted*
12 heaping Tbsps. Romano
* cheese, freshly grated*

Place olive oil and butter in a large skillet and heat until butter is melted, being careful not to burn the butter. Add onions and sauté until onions are transparent. Transfer onions to a large saucepan and add beef stock, cover, and simmer over low heat until onions are tender, about 15 minutes. Pour into six individual oven-proof casseroles. Stir one tablespoon Dry Sherry into each casserole, add toasted French bread and top each slice with two heaping tablespoons Romano cheese. Place the casseroles in a preheated 350° oven until cheese is melted, about five minutes. Serves 6.

SUMMER SOUP

1 32 oz. can tomato juice, chilled
2 Tbsps. red wine vinegar
3 Tbsps. sugar
1 tsp. Tobasco sauce
4 Tbsps. Dry Vermouth
Cucumber, very thinly sliced,
* to taste*
Celery, chopped, to taste
Carrots, sliced in very thin
* slivers, to taste*
Green onions, finely chopped, to
* taste*
Salt, to taste

Notes from Patti:

Just as there is no substitute for Sherry, there is no substitute for Vermouth.

To tomato juice add vinegar, sugar, Tobasco, Dry Vermouth, cucumber, celery, carrot, green onions, and salt to taste. Serve very cold with one ice cube in each bowl. Summer soup should be prepared several hours prior to serving to realize the perfect marriage of flavors. Serves 6.

RED CABBAGE SOUP

Soup:

*1½ lbs. beef chuck, cut into
    small chunks*
2 soup bones
1 large onion, coarsely chopped
1 Tbsp. salt
1 tsp. pepper
*6 ripe, fresh tomatoes, peeled
    and seeded (must be fresh!)*
*4 large fresh beets, peeled and
sliced*
1 bay leaf
*1 large red cabbage, coarsely
    shredded*
*3 large potatoes, peeled and
    quartered*
Juice of 2 lemons
4 Tbsps. Cream Sherry

Garnish:

1½ Tbsps. fresh dill, chopped

Place meat, bones, onion, salt and pepper in large pot; add a minimum of 4 quarts water to cover. Bring to slow boil, skimming all fat from surface. Add tomatoes, beets, and bay leaf. Simmer, partially covered, 1½ hours. Add cabbage, potatoes, and lemon juice. Simmer, partially covered, 1 hour. Add Cream Sherry. Cool, remove bones. Refrigerate 24 hours to allow flavors to fully blend. Remove solidified fat off the top and reheat. Sprinkle with dill just before serving. Serves 6 generously.

BARBERA BEAN SOUP

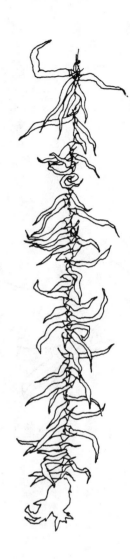

Soup:

1 cup dried red beans
1 cup dried lentils
1½ quarts water
1½ cups Barbera*
2 large onions, coarsely chopped
3 stalks celery, coarsely chopped
3 carrots, coarsely grated
4-5 cloves garlic, finely minced
2 Tbsps. red wine vinegar
½ cup barley
1 can tomato paste
1 bay leaf
2 Tbsps. olive oil

Seasonings: (to taste)

Oregano
Chili powder
Cayenne
Salt and pepper

Soak beans and lentils in large pot overnight in the water.

Add remaining soup ingredients and bring to boil; turn heat to low and simmer 1½ hours covered. Add seasonings to taste. Cook another 45 minutes. Serves 6 hearty appetites.

*Zinfandel may be substituted for Barbera.

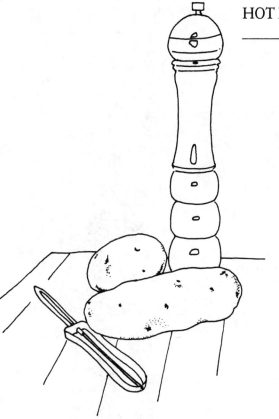

HOT POTATO, COLD POTATO SOUP

Soup:

*3 large potatoes, peeled and
   cubed*
2 large onions, coarsely chopped
*4-5 chicken bouillon cubes, dis-
   solved in 2 cups of boiling
   water*
1 cube (¼ lb.) butter
2 Tbsps. lemon juice
¾ cup dry French Colombard*
Salt and white pepper, to taste
*1 cup evaporated milk or light
   cream (when soup is served
   hot)*

Garnish:

Fresh dill, or
Fresh parsley, or
Pimento

Place all ingredients into *heavy pot* and add just enough additional water to cover. Cook until the potatoes are mushy. Cool -- pour into blender or food processor fitted with a chopping blade. Blend until very smooth. Chill and serve cold, or serve hot, adding the milk or cream when reheating. Garnish with any of the following: fresh dill, fresh parsley, pimento. Serves 6.

*Johannisberg Riesling may be substituted for the French Colombard.

Vegetables

I grew up eating home-grown vegetables and always had a garden until a few years ago. Everything was picked the same day it was eaten or canned. My Grandmother, for example, believed that there was only one way to cook corn on the cob. She'd put a big kettle of salted water on the stove and would turn up the flame. Then she and I would pick the corn and shuck it. By then the water would be at a rolling boil and in would go those golden cobs to be timed exactly 1 minute. Nothing ever tasted so good!

Today many vegetables, such as tomatoes, are developed for mechanical harvesters and have little flavor. If you have any space at all, I encourage you to plant a garden. It doesn't take a lot of room, it's good exercise, and the rewards are boundless. If you cannot have a garden, then at least buy those vegetables that are in season in your area. When preparing them, don't hesitate to mix two or more vegetables together. Above all else, DO NOT OVERCOOK. Those who show appreciation for some of nature's more nutritious gifts will find great taste and beautiful colors that add yet another dimension to your dining pleasure.

PATRICK'S ONION FLAN

Most people like onions. My son Patrick *loves* onions. He eats them like apples. Eggs without onions aren't good eggs; peanut butter and onion sandwiches, and on, and on. I used to buy onions the way other people bought potatoes -- by the 10 pound bag! On Patrick's 12th birthday I asked him what he would like for dinner. He said he didn't care as long as there were lots of onions in it. Since I couldn't figure out a recipe for an onion cake, I devised this flan instead. He still asks for his onion flan on his birthday.

Pastry:

1¼ cups flour
6 Tbsps. (¾ cube) butter, cut in
   small pieces
2 Tbsps. vegetable shortening
⅛ tsp. salt
¼ tsp. sugar
3 Tbsps. cold water
1 10" flan ring

Filling:

¼ cup (½ cube) butter
2 Tbsps. olive oil
6 cups onions, thinly sliced
2 cloves garlic, finely minced
2 Tbsps. Dry Sherry
16 anchovy fillets, cut in half
   lengthwise
24 black olives, pitted

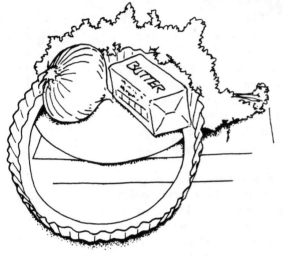

Notes from Patti:

Flan rings are a circular shape with the ends welded together and no bottom. They can be smooth sided or fluted and range in sizes from 3½" to 10½". Place the ring on a cookie sheet and gently fit the rolled dough into the ring. With a sharp knife cut off the surplus dough following the contour of ring around the top.

Place all pastry ingredients except the water in a large mixing bowl. Toss, using hands and with fingers blend the mixture until cohesive, but still a bit lumpy. Add water and mix until smooth or, using the food processor method, place all ingredients except the water in the bowl fitted with a chopping blade. Process on and off until mixture has the consistency of small peas. While machine is running, add the water through the feed tube and process until dough is smooth. Form a ball and wrap dough in plastic wrap. Refrigerate ½ hour, then roll and fit into flan ring. Chill while preparing filling.

Place a ¼ cup butter and olive oil in large skillet and heat until butter is melted, add onions and garlic and sauté until onion is transparent. Add Dry Sherry and continue to cook until onions are a light golden color. Pour into pastry lined flan ring. Arrange anchovy fillets, lattice fashion, over onion mixture. Press 1 olive into each square. Bake 30 minutes in 375° oven. Serves 4.

CARCIOFFI FRITTATA

2 6 oz. jars marinated artichokes
    (reserve 2-3 Tbsps. artichoke
    marinade)
1 small white onion, peeled and
    finely chopped
¼ lb. mushrooms, finely
    chopped
2 Tbsps. Dry Sherry
4 large eggs, well beaten
6-8 saltine crackers, coarsely
    crumbled
½ lb. sharp cheddar cheese,
    coarsely grated
2 Tbsps. parsley, finely chopped
1 tsp. Tabasco sauce

Notes from Patti:

For a luncheon dish, pour in-to four 8''x 4'' au gratin dishes and bake in a 350° oven for 30-35 minutes. This is easy, elegant and rich; for that reason I would serve only fresh rolls and butter with a crisp Pinot Blanc or one of the drier Chenin Blancs.

Drain artichokes, and cut in fourths. Place 2-3 tablespoons artichoke marinade in a small skillet and lightly sauté onions and mushrooms. Add Dry Sherry and cook until liquid is reduced to half. Place eggs in a large mixing bowl and fold in crackers, cheese, parsley, Tabasco sauce, sautéed onion and mushrooms. Pour mixture into a 9''x 14'' pan and bake in a 350° oven for 40 minutes. Cool and cut into squares. Serves 8 to 10.

There are many advantages to working at Bargetto Winery. Good wine, good friends and not least of all, good food.

We are fortunate that Patti Ballard loves to cook and even better, enjoys sharing her culinary skills with her friends and co-workers.

One of my favorite dishes is her Carcioffi Frittata. While similar to a quiche it is lighter but richer and satisfying.

I'm sure your family and friends will enjoy this savory fare as much as we do at the winery.

Judy Giggy, Sales Room Supervisor
Bargetto Winery

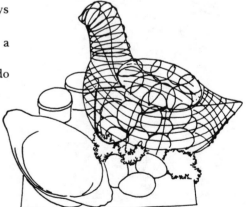

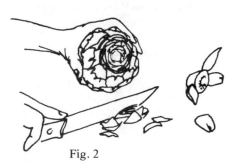

Fig. 1

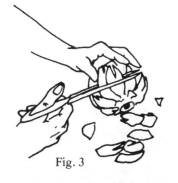

Fig. 2

Fig. 3

EASY ARTICHOKE MOUSSE

This is very good served hot with a simple tarragon sauce or cold as a luncheon dish. This can also be baked in a long shallow pan and cut into bite size pieces to be served as antipasto.

> 2 9 oz. packages frozen
>   artichokes
> ⅓ cup heavy cream
> Salt, to taste
> 1 cup unflavored bread crumbs
> ⅓ cup milk
> 6 green onions, including green
>   tops, finely minced
> 5 Tbsps. butter
> 5 large eggs
> ¾ tsp. black pepper, freshly
>   ground
> 1 tsp. nutmeg, freshly ground or
>   grated

Prepare artichokes according to package directions and drain thoroughly. Place artichokes and ⅓ cup heavy cream in a blender or a food processor fitted with chopping blade and puree until smooth. Add salt to taste and blend another 10 seconds.

Mix the bread crumbs with ⅓ cup milk. Then squeeze through a double thickness of cheesecloth to remove all moisture. Set aside.

Sauté the green onions in butter until just transparent. Add artichoke pureé and stir for a minute or two. Add bread crumbs and stir thoroughly. Beat eggs in the blender or food processor; add artichoke puree, pepper and nutmeg and blend thoroughly.

Butter and flour a two quart mold. Fill with mixture. Set the mold in a shallow pan filled with boiling water about ⅓ of the way up the side of the mold. Bake in 375° preheated oven 30-35 minutes or until the top is set and the mixture pulls away from the sides. Serves 6.

HOW TO PREPARE AND COOK ARTICHOKES

Cut off stems at base of artichokes, turn on side and cut off the top of the artichoke. Starting with bottom leaves, snip off the top of each leaf with sharp kitchen shears. Stand artichokes upright in a deep saucepan large enough for the artichokes to fit snugly in the pan. Add 3'' boiling water, 1½ teaspoons salt, 2 tablespoons olive oil and 1 tablespoon lemon juice. Cover and boil gently for ½ hour or until the base can be pierced easily. Turn artichokes upside down to drain. If artichokes are to be stuffed, gently spread the leaves and scrape out the choke (the fuzzy stuff), to make room for stuffing (see figures 1-7).

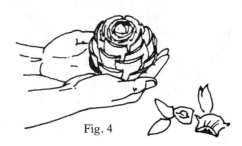

Fig. 4

ARTICHOKES ITALIAN

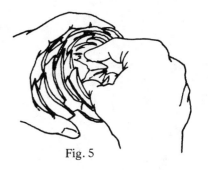

Fig. 5

When I'm writing and need to get away from telephones and interruptions, I head straight to my friends, Bernie and Priscilla Smith, of South Lake Tahoe. Although I work hard while I'm there, we always find time to relax. On one working visit, I prepared a picnic, and Bernie took us out in his boat to the middle of Emerald Bay where he dropped anchor. We lunched on pate with homemade French bread, and these wonderful stuffed artichokes, served with a perfectly chilled magnum of fine California Champagne. Of course, there was not a crumb or a sip of anything left.

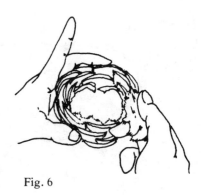

Fig. 6

6 medium artichokes, prepared
by basic directions, dechoked,
and chilled
1 cup olive oil
½ cup red wine vinegar
¼ cup water
1 Tbsp. salt
1 tsp. sugar
¾ tsp. oregano, crushed
¾ tsp. basil, crushed
1 tsp. dry mustard
¼ tsp. pepper
3 large cloves garlic, finely
minced
Small head cauliflower, cut into
small flowerettes
½ lb. fresh mushrooms, thickly
sliced
2 medium carrots, thickly
sliced
½ cup sliced ripe olives
12 thin slices salami, cut in strips
1 7 oz. can tuna, well drained

Fig. 7

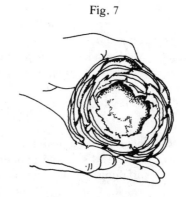

Notes from Patti:

This is one of the most versatile recipes in this book. It is a delight to the eye as well as to the palate. Use this as a salad or the main course. I like to use smaller artichokes for salads. Save the leftover vegetable mixture for another day. As the main course use larger artichokes. A good, hearty California red wine, like Petite Sirah or Barbera, would be my wine choice.

Pour the olive oil, vinegar, water, salt, sugar, oregano, basil, dry mustard, pepper and garlic in a large sauce pan. Bring to boiling point and boil for 5 minutes. Add cauliflower, mushrooms, and carrots, and bring back to boiling point. Boil 3 minutes (no longer). Cool to room temperature and chill 3 to 4 hours. Drain vegetables, reserving marinade. Combine vegetables, olives, salami and tuna. Place artichokes on individual plates. Spoon mixture into the center of artichokes and circle the artichoke with more of the mixture. Be sure to place a server of the marinade on the table for your guests. Serves 6.

POTATO GNOCCHI

Gnocchi (pronounced nyo-ki), is sometimes served in place of pasta in the meal.

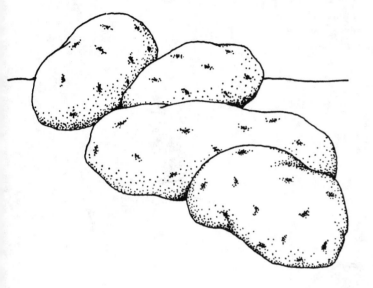

Gnocchi:

6 large potatoes, boiled in their
* skins and peeled*
6 Tbsps. butter, at room tem-
* perature*
3 large eggs, lightly beaten
2 tsps. baking powder
Salt and pepper, to taste
4 cups flour, sifted once
6 quarts water
1 Tbsps. salt

To Bake:

6 Tbsps. butter, melted
½ cup freshly grated parmesan
* cheese*

Mash potatoes with the 6 tablespoons butter. Add eggs and baking powder and beat well. Add salt and pepper to taste. Blend in flour, a little at a time, making a stiff dough. Knead until dough is smooth. Shape dough into long rolls about ½'' thick. Cut into 1'' pieces. Lightly flour hands and roll pieces into balls. Bring 6 quarts of water to a rolling boil, add the 1 tablespoon salt. Drop a few gnocchi balls into the water and cook until they rise to the top. Remove with slotted spoon to paper toweling and drain. Continue until all gnocchi are cooked.

Pour 2 tablespoons of the melted butter into a shallow baking dish to cover the bottom and sides. Arrange the gnocchi in a single layer. Drizzle the rest of the melted butter over the top and top with the Parmesan cheese. Bake in a pre-heated 400° oven for about 5 minutes or until cheese is melted. Serves 6 generously.

CORN PUDDING

This is so simple to make -- like many of the simple dishes of our mothers' and grandmothers' time. This one is seldom seen today. Test to see if done as you would a custard, by inserting a knife which comes out clean if done.

1 14½ oz. can cream style corn
3 large eggs, well beaten
2 cups milk, scalded
3 Tbsps. Dry Sherry
2 Tbsps. butter, melted
Salt and pepper, to taste

Mix all ingredients and pour into a buttered casserole dish. Bake, uncovered, 1½ hours in 300° oven. Serves 4.

SHIRLEY'S BRUSSEL SPROUTS

There is a jewel of a lady in my life named Shirley Davis who understands my Gemini personality perfectly. She knows I like a place for everything and everything in its place; windows always sparkling, the top of the refrigerator never dusty and closets and cabinets perpetually neat. Linens without wrinkles, magazines neatly stacked, ashtrays always clean and copper cookware polished to outshine the sun. Now I would like you to believe that I am a busy lady who doesn't really have the time to take care of these domestic engineering problems, and therefore my need of Shirley's expert help. But Shirley knows the *real* truth!

These are for people who really hate brussel sprouts!

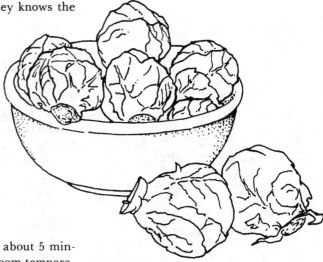

2 lbs. brussel sprouts
½ cup olive oil
¼ cup red wine vinegar
2-3 cloves garlic, finely minced
   (I like more!)
½ tsp. rosemary, finely crushed
¼ tsp. oregano, finely crushed
1 tsp. dill weed
Salt and pepper, to taste
⅓ cup parsley finely minced

Remove any tough outer leaves and par–boil brussel sprouts about 5 minutes, being careful not to overcook. Drain thoroughly and cool at room temperature. Toss with remaining ingredients. Refrigerate in covered container 24 hours before serving. This keeps and keeps! Serves 6 to 8.

HOT-STUFFED CHILIS

Pamela Kittler, a free-lance food columnist, has had a wide and varied experience in both the food and wine industries; working, for example, in the planning and preparation of VIP meals at a large California winery. Our association is a particularly happy one as we share the same enthusiasm for good food that is easily prepared, but always elegant. As my editor, she has made a major contribution to this book. This is her recipe for a hot and spicy appetizer.

Chilis:

24 small (2'') fresh, mild yellow chilis, or
8 large (6''-7'') fresh, mild green chilis

Filling:

1 16 oz. can crabmeat
½ cup Jack or Swiss cheese, grated
1 13 oz. package cream cheese,
*   softened*
2 Tbsps. Dry Sherry
2 Tbsps. green onions, finely chopped
1 Tbsp. parsley, finely chopped
Nutmeg, salt and pepper, to
*   taste*

Batter:

3 eggs, separated
3 Tbsps. flour
⅛ tsp. salt
Oil for frying

Cut the tops off of the chilis and seed them. Rinse under cold water and set aside.

Blend all the filling ingredients together in a blender or food processor fitted with a chopping blade until well mixed, but not completely smooth. Stuff reserved chilis with the crab mixture using either your fingers or a pastry bag. If you are using the large chilis, slice them into 1''-2'' pieces after stuffing.

Blend the 3 egg yolks together with the flour until smooth. Beat the 3 egg whites with the salt until very stiff. Gently mix in ¼ of the beaten whites into the yolk mixture, then fold the yolk mixture completely into the remaining beaten whites. Heat 1'' of oil in a frying pan until a haze forms. Dip and coat the chilis or chili pieces in the batter and fry, a few at a time, until brown, turning once. Drain and keep warm until frying is complete. Serve hot as hors d'-oeuvres or as a first course, topped with a light tomato sauce flavored with fresh cilantro. Makes 2 dozen.

MUSHROOMS IN FOIL

4 cups fresh mushrooms, thickly
   sliced
4 Tbsps. butter
4 tsps. lemon juice
8 Tbsps. Dry Sherry
4 double thick pieces of foil large
   enough to seal each serving

Place 1 cup of the sliced mushrooms on double thick foil piece — sprinkle with 1 teaspoon lemon juice, 2 tablespoons Sherry, and dot with 1 tablespoon butter. Seal and bake 15 minutes in 350° oven. Serves 4.

Notes from Patti:

"Mushrooms in Foil" is very good with broiled steaks or rare roasts, especially with *Mustard Roast*, (see page 93). Just pop them in the oven with the roast during the last 10 minutes of baking time. The heat inside the foil will finish the last 5 minutes of cooking (15 minutes cooking altogether).

CLAM STUFFED MUSHROOMS

24 large mushrooms
1 6 oz. can minced clams (reserve juices)
½ lb. ricotta cheese
½ cup green onions including
   green tops, finely chopped
2 large cloves garlic, finely
   minced
½ tsp. fresh rosemary
¼ cup parsley, finely chopped
1 cup Parmesan cheese, freshly
   grated
½ cup fresh bread crumbs
½ cup Johannisberg Riesling*
½ cup butter, melted (must be
   butter!)

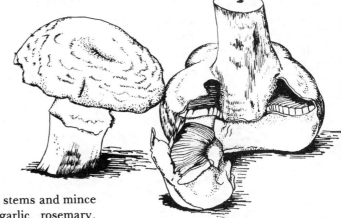

Wipe mushrooms with damp paper towel and dry. Remove stems and mince them finely. Combine chopped stems with green onions, garlic, rosemary, clams, bread crumbs, ricotta cheese and ½ cup of the Parmesan cheese. Stuff caps with mixture. Arrange caps in glass baking dish, sprinkle with parsley and remaining Parmesan. Drizzle butter over all. Mix Johannisberg Riesling and reserved clam juice and pour around mushrooms. Cover and bake 35 minutes at 375°. Serves 4.

*Fumé Blanc (Sauvignon Blanc) may be substituted for the Johannisberg Riesling.

GRANDMA'S BEST MUSHROOMS

Pay attention when you buy mushrooms. Make sure the caps have not pulled away from stems. If mushrooms are dark brown -- *AVOID!!* (some mushrooms are naturally *light* brown. It depends on the compost used for growing).

Never wash mushrooms -- always wipe with damp paper towels.

Never overcook -- especially with soups, stews, and sauces, where the mushrooms can be added when cooking is finished, allowing heat to do the rest.

Mushrooms will stay fresh and white for a good week and a half if covered with damp paper towels (leave them in paper box-not plastic bags!)

If you are fortunate to have a mushroom farm in your town, take advantage of it -- much better quality and cheaper!

This is a great brunch dish and takes 10 minutes at the most. Serve over hot, buttered toast.

> ½ cup tomato sauce
> ¼ cup olive oil
> ¼ cup Dry Sherry
> ⅛ tsp. cayenne pepper
> 2 tsps. dry mustard
> Salt and pepper, to taste
> 1½ lbs. fresh mushrooms, cut
>   into fourths
> ½ cup heavy cream

Pour tomato sauce, olive oil, Dry Sherry, cayenne pepper and dry mustard into a large, heavy skillet. Heat, add salt and pepper to taste. Cover, reduce heat and simmer about 3 minutes. Add cream and stir well. Add mushrooms and stir to coat with sauce. Cover, bring to a boil, reduce heat and simmer 2-3 minutes. Serves 6.

MIXED-UP SQUASH

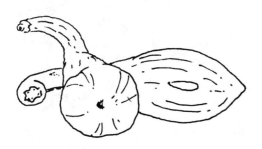

> 2 Tbsps. olive oil
> 2 Tbsps. butter
> 1 large onion, coarsely minced
> ½ large red sweet pepper, finely
>   minced
> 1 lb. zucchini, thinly sliced
> 1 lb. summer squash, thinly
>   sliced
> 1 lb. yellow crookneck squash,
>   thickly sliced
> ½ cup French Columbard*
> ¼ tsp. basil
> Salt and pepper, to taste

Heat olive oil and butter in large, heavy skillet. Add onions and peppers and saute until onions are transparent. Add squash, French Colombard, basil and salt and pepper to taste, Lower flame and simmer, uncovered, 15 minutes. Serves 6.

*Johannisberg Riesling may be substituted for French Colombard.

BAKED SPINACH

2 large bunches spinach, washed
    and dried
2 Tbsps. parsley, finely minced
2 Tbsps. olive oil
½ pint Ricotta cheese
3 Tbsps. Dry Sherry
4 large eggs, well beaten
1 cup sharp cheddar cheese,
    grated
1 cup milk
Salt and pepper, to taste
2 Tbsps. butter

Tear spinach in large pieces, discarding large stems. In a large skillet, sauté in the olive oil. Stir in the parsley.

In an 8''x 8'' baking dish blend Ricotta, Dry Sherry, eggs and cheddar cheese. Add sautééd spinach and parsley, the milk, and salt and pepper to taste. Stir once or twice. Dot with butter. Bake 45 minutes in 350° oven. serves 6.

Notes from Patti:

Always place cheeses, especially softer cheeses, in freezer for an hour before grating either with a food processor or by hand. This prevents the cheese from crumbling. If you need only a small amount of cheese, don't forget your handy, dandy potato peeler!

ZUCCHINI PANCAKES
(Food Processor Method)

The bright green color of these pancakes makes them a great side dish to unadorned meat or poultry. And they're a snap with the help of a food processor.

3 large, unpeeled zucchini, very
    coarsely grated
2 large eggs
4 Tbsps. flour
2 Tbsps. Parmesan cheese,
    freshly grated
2 Tbsps. green onions, including
    green tops, grated
½ tsp. parsley, chopped
Dash garlic powder
2 Tbsps. Dry Sherry
Salt and pepper, to taste

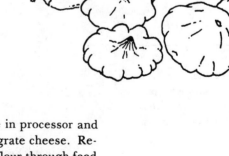

Cut the zucchini to fit the feed tube. Place grating blade in processor and grate zucchini and green onions. Remove to mixing bowl and grate cheese. Replace grating blade with chopping blade and blend eggs. Add flour through feed tube and blend. Return all other grated ingredients and add garlic powder, Dry Sherry and salt and pepper to taste to processor and blend, using on/off method. Drop one tablespoon of the mixture at a time into well oiled skillet. Fry over medium heat and turn until golden brown on both sides. Makes 18 pancakes.

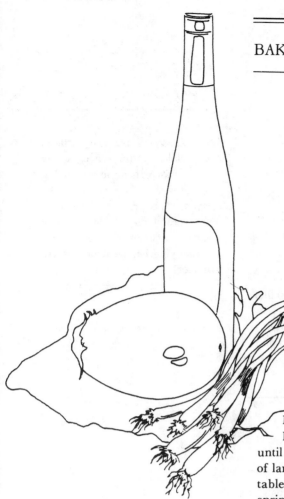

BAKED ZUCCHINI AND EGGPLANT

Vegetables:

2 large onions, coarsely chopped
2 large cloves garlic, finely minced
5 Tbsps. olive oil
2 medium zucchini, thickly sliced
2 green peppers, cored and cut in wide strips
2 fresh, firm tomatoes, thickly sliced
1 large eggplant, peeled and
    thinly sliced
¼ cup Dry Vermouth

Seasonings:

1 Tbsp. salt
¼ tsp. ground pepper
1 tsp. oregano
¼ tsp. cumin
¼ tsp. dill weed

Mix the seasonings together.
In a large skillet, sauté onions and garlic in 2 tablespoons of the olive oil until onions are transparent. Place half the suatéed onions and garlic in bottom of large casserole. Add zucchini and ⅓ of mixed seasonings. Sprinkle with 1 tablespoon olive oil. Add eggplant, sprinkle with ⅓ of mixed seasonings and sprinkle with 1 tablespoon olive oil. Add green peppers and remaining seasonings. Sprinkle with last tablespoon olive oil. Pour the Dry Vermouth over all. Bake, uncovered, 1 hour in 350% oven. Top with tomatoes and remaining sautéed onion and garlic. Bake, uncovered, 15 minutes more. Serves 6.

ONION BROCCOLI

Notes from Patti:

Don't discard the stems of broccoli. Simply peel them and cook with the broccoli. After peeling they will not be tough or stringy.

1 large bunch broccoli
¼ cup (½ cube) butter, melted
½ envelope dry onion/mush-
    room soup mix
3 Tbsps. lemon juice
2 Tbsps. Dry Sherry
1 cup Cheddar cheese, grated

Steam broccoli 7 minutes, drain thoroughly and place in a baking dish. Sprinkle butter, onion mushroom soup mix, lemon juice and Dry Sherry evenly over the broccoli. Top with cheese. Place under the broiler until cheese melts and is slightly browned. Serves 4.

SHERRY CARROTS

2 lbs. carrots (made into little
    carrots)
3 Tbsps. butter (must be butter)
Salt and white pepper, to taste
1 heaping Tbsp. dark brown
    sugar
¾ cup Dry Sherry
1 Tbsp. parsley finely minced

Melt butter in large skillet and sauté carrots until well coated with butter, turning often. Salt and pepper to taste, add Sherry, and simmer, covered, 5 to 6 minutes. Remove lid, add brown sugar and mash it into the Sherry. Turn carrots several times to be sure all the carrots are well glazed. Sprinkle with parsley before serving. Serves 6.

CABBAGE BARBERA

1 medium red cabbage, finely
    shredded
2 Tbsps. salt
½ cup onions, finely chopped
½ cup green pepper, finely
    chopped
⅓ cup parsley, finely chopped
½ cup Barbera*
¼ cup red wine vinegar
½ cup olive oil
3 small cloves garlic, crushed
3-4 tsps. sugar
1 tsp. dry mustard

Notes from Patti:

This recipe is a snap with a food processor. Use a chopping blade and chop onions, green peppers, parsley and garlic, turning on/off 4 times. Add Barbera, vinegar, olive oil, sugar and dry mustard and turn on/off 2-3 times. Add to cabbage prepared as in basic recipe.

Put cabbage in *large* bowl lined with several layers of paper towels. Add salt and mix thoroughly. Cover with 4-5 layers of paper towels. Refrigerate 3-4 hours. Remove any liquid. Place cabbage in terry cloth towel and press until *all* liquid has been removed. Mix remaining ingredients well. Pour over cabbage. Refrigerate 2-3 hours. Serves 6 to 8.
*Pinot Noir may be substituted for the Barbera.

SWEET AND SOUR CABBAGE

This dish should *always* be made a day in advance, and is, therefore, ideal for larger dinner parties. Guests always seem surprised to be served cabbage until they taste. Great served in chafing dish.

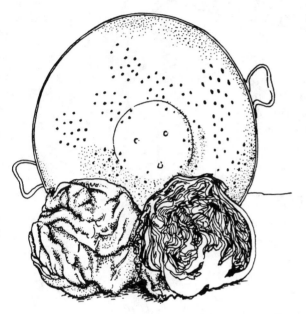

4 thick slices smoked bacon, cut
* in small pieces*
1 large onion, coarsely chopped
2 large heads red cabbage,
* shredded*
2 cloves garlic, finely minced
1 Tbsp. caraway seeds
1 cup boiling water
Salt and pepper, to taste
2 large pears, peeled, cored and
* cut into large chunks*
1 large lemon, cut in fourths and
* seeded*
2 cups Cabernet Sauvignon*
2 Tbsps. red wine vinegar
2 Tbsps. honey

Cook bacon in large dutch oven, until nicely browned. Add onions and cook until transparent. Drain all but 2 tablespoons of the fat. Add cabbage, garlic, caraway seeds and the boiling water. Cover and cook until cabbage wilts. Add pears, lemon pieces, Cabernet Sauvignon, and vinegar, and salt and pepper to taste. Cover and cook 10 minutes on medium heat. Add honey and stir thoroughly. Cover and cook on *very low* heat for ½ hour. Remove lemon and continue to cook until cabbage is reduced to half the original amount. If not sweet-sour enough, add a little brown sugar -- liquid should be about 1''. If more set lid ajar to reduce while cooking. Cool to room temperature. Refrigerate for 24 hours. Heat just before serving. Serves 6.
*Pinot Noir may be substituted for the Cabernet Sauvignon.

EGGPLANT PARMIGIANA WITH ZINFANDEL

Vegetables:

*1 medium eggplant, peeled and
  sliced ¼'' thick*
2 large eggs
½ cup Parmesan cheese, grated
Flour for dredging
Corn oil for frying
*¾ cup Mozzarella cheese, cut in
  small cubes*
*3 slices Prosciutto (Italian ham),
  chopped*

Sauce:

*1 medium onion, coarsely
  chopped*
3 Tbsps. olive oil
*2 cups tomatoes, seeded and
  chopped*
½ cup Zinfandel*
Salt and pepper, to taste

Notes from Patti:

It has been said that at Roman Banquets parsley was worn by the diners like a laurel wreath to ward off the dangers of intoxication.

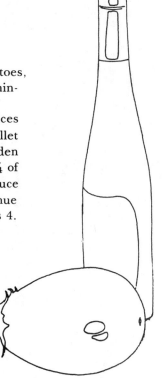

   Prepare sauce: Sauté onions in olive oil until transparent. Add tomatoes, Zinfandel, oregano, basil, parsley, salt and pepper to taste. Simmer for 20 minutes or so.
   Beat eggs with 2 tablespoons of the Parmesan cheese. Dip eggplant slices in egg mixture, then dredge in flour. Pour enough corn oil in large heavy skillet for browning. Drop eggplant slices, one at a time, in *HOT* oil. Cook until golden brown. Drain on paper towels. Continue until all eggplant is cooked. Pour ¼ of the sauce in large casserole. Add layer of eggplant, sprinkle with more sauce and some of the Mozzarella, Prosciutto, and remaining Parmesan. Continue layers. Top with sauce, cover and bake 20-30 minutes in 400º oven. Serves 4.
   *Cabernet Sauvignon may be substituted for Zinfandel.

Pasta

Pasta is automatically thought of as Italian, and rightly so, since the theory of Marco Polo bringing pasta from China has long since been disproved. We know, for instance, that the Italians were enjoying pasta in 1279. But it matters little who discovered it or where it originated. It is enough that man discovered the infinite possibilities of grain as a versatile and nourishing food. Pasta ranges from very simple dishes to complicated creations. It's served with almost anything from soup to nuts. In some parts of Italy macaroni is even stuffed with honey and sprinkled with sugar for dessert.

The pasta of today is much different and much improved from the pasta of the 13th century. There is, however, still little of the commercial pasta that I will use. I prefer homemade pasta, not just because it has a better flavor and texture, but because the creation of a dish so good from such simple and natural foods is most satisfying. It isn't necessary to have a pasta machine to make good pasta, but it makes the task easier. There are many types on the market ranging in price from $15 to $200 for an electric model. I have my Grandmother's machine and use it constantly. With or without a machine, homemade pasta is well worth the time it takes to prepare.

TECHNIQUES FOR MAKING AND
COOKING HANDMADE PASTA

All pasta doughs are made with a varying ratio of flour to eggs; the larger the proportion of eggs, the richer the pasta. It is best made with Semolina, a type of wheat flour. If Semolina flour is not available, by all means use unbleached, all purpose flour. Never use instant or self-rising flour, as these cause the pasta to separate and break apart during cooking. Temperature is also an important factor when making pasta. A moderate room temperature, away from drafts is best. A marble slab is the ideal surface for making and rolling pasta, but any smooth surface will do. Pasta can be mixed directly on the work surface, the way I prefer, or in a large bowl. The technique is the same.

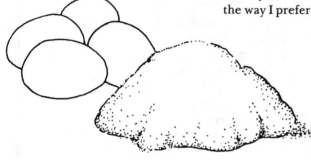

Pasta Dough:

3½ *cups flour*
5 *eggs, room-temperature*
1 *Tbsp. olive oil (more, if neces-*
   sary, to make dough cohesive,
   but dry)
½ *tsp. salt*

Makes 1 pound, enough to serve 4.

Pour flour on work surface, or into a large bowl and form a well in the center. Beat the eggs, olive oil and salt, pour into the well. Mix the flour, a little at a time, with your fingers, starting from inside the well until eggs and flour are well blended. Knead the dough, pressing it with the heel of your hand and folding it several times until the pasta becomes smooth and elastic. This takes about 10 minutes. Wrap the dough in a damp cloth and allow it to rest for ½ hour to 45 minutes.

Divide the dough in half, keeping the remaining half covered, to prevent drying. Lightly flour the work surface and begin by rolling the dough away from you, turning the dough one quarter and repeating the procedure so the dough keeps an ever circular shape. If any section becomes sticky, dust very lightly with flour. Carefully stretch the dough as you roll it and roll until it is almost paper thin. Roll up the dough on your rolling pin and unroll on a clean, dry cloth. Place it on the work surface (a little will hang over the edge.) Rotate after 15 minutes. Be sure to time the drying period or the dough will become overdried. Fold it over and over into a roll about 3'' wide. Slice into noodles. After cutting the noodles, open them on a clean, dry cloth and allow to dry at least another 15 minutes. If using a pasta machine, follow manufacturer's instructions.

You cannot use too much water to cook pasta -- at least 6 quarts per pound. Bring water to a rolling boil, add 1 tablespoon salt, 2 tablespoons oil and the pasta. Cook about 5 minutes or until "al dente", which means tender but still slightly resistant to the bite. The more you make pasta the easier it becomes, so practice, practice, practice!

Notes from Patti:

A food processor can be used to make the dough. Insert a chopping blade, add all ingredients at the same time and using the on/off method, process until dough forms a ball.

SPAGHETTI WITH CLAM SAUCE

3 cloves garlic, finely minced
¼ cup olive oil
3 Tbsps. flour
2 cups clam juice
½ cup Pinot Blanc
2 cups clams, finely minced
2 Tbsps. parsley, finely minced
Salt and pepper, to taste
½ lb. spaghetti

Pour oil in a large skillet. Add garlic and cook until transparent. Blend in the flour; add clam juice and Pinot Blanc and cook over low heat until slightly thickened. Simmer 10 minutes. Add clams, parsley and salt and pepper to taste. Cover and simmer 5 minutes.

While sauce is simmering, cook spaghetti al dente and drain thoroughly. Pour sauce over spaghetti and toss until all the pasta is well coated. Serves 2. (This recipe can easily be doubled.)

Notes from Patti:

There is a tendency to over-cook pasta in this country, giving it a limp, pasty consistency. Al dente is the Italian phrase for cooking it until just done: tender, yet still a bit resistent to the bite.

NUTTY SPAGHETTI

2 Tbsps. olive oil
4 Tbsps. butter
2 large cloves garlic, finely
  minced
¼ cup walnuts, coarsely chopped
¼ cup pine nuts, coarsely
  chopped
¼ cup Chenin Blanc
¼ cup white raisins
Salt and pepper, to taste
½ lb. spaghetti
½ cup Romano cheese, freshly
  grated

In a large skillet heat 2 tablespoons of the butter and the olive oil until a slight haze forms. Add garlic, walnuts and pine nuts. Cook over medium heat about 4 minutes, stirring constantly. Add Chenin Blanc and raisins and continue to cook 2-3 minutes. Add salt and pepper to taste.

Meanwhile, cook the spaghetti in 3 quarts of salted water until al dente. Drain in large colander. Toss spaghetti in the skillet with sauce and the remaining 2 tablespoons butter until spaghetti is well coated and butter is melted. Sprinkle with the Romano cheese and toss again. Serve at once. Serves 2. (This recipe can easily be doubled.)

Notes from Patti:

Pine nuts are the edible seeds of the Pine tree. History doesn't tell us who the smart person was who discovered their great food value and their even greater flavor. We do know, however, that pine nuts have been used in European cooking for hundreds of years -- especially in Italian foods. In some areas of northern Italy, meat is scarce and the pine nut has become a substitute.

LADIES OF THE NIGHT SPAGHETTI

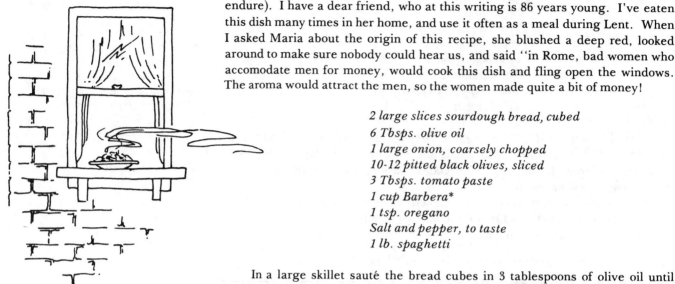

There is quite a story about this recipe (as there is about most recipes that endure). I have a dear friend, who at this writing is 86 years young. I've eaten this dish many times in her home, and use it often as a meal during Lent. When I asked Maria about the origin of this recipe, she blushed a deep red, looked around to make sure nobody could hear us, and said "in Rome, bad women who accomodate men for money, would cook this dish and fling open the windows. The aroma would attract the men, so the women made quite a bit of money!

2 large slices sourdough bread, cubed
6 Tbsps. olive oil
1 large onion, coarsely chopped
10-12 pitted black olives, sliced
3 Tbsps. tomato paste
1 cup Barbera*
1 tsp. oregano
Salt and pepper, to taste
1 lb. spaghetti

In a large skillet sauté the bread cubes in 3 tablespoons of olive oil until nicely browned. Remove and keep warm in oven. Add remaining 3 tablespoons of olive oil to pan and sauté onions and olives until the onion is transparent. Blend in the 3 tablespoons tomato paste and oregano into the Barbera and pour it into the onions and olives. Salt and pepper to taste, turn heat low and simmer for 10-12 minutes. Meanwhile cook spaghetti in about 6 quarts boiling salted water until al dente. Drain in colander and add to sauce, tossing until the spaghetti is well coated. Add bread cubes and serve at once. Serves 4.

* Pinot Noir may be substituted for the Barbera.

POLENTA

Polenta, in one form or another, is one of the oldest foods in the world. It is the "pasta" of Northern Italy: very simple, but filling and nutritious. Eat it with melted butter and grated cheese or pour marinara sauce over it.

1½ quarts water
2 tsps. salt
1½ cups yellow corn meal

Bring water and salt to a rolling boil in a heavy 4 quart pan. Pour the cornmeal very slowly into the boiling water, making sure that the boiling never stops. Stir constantly to prevent the cornmeal from lumping. Reduce heat to very low and continue to cook another 25-30 minutes. Stir very often to prevent sticking or burning. Serves 4.

Notes from Patti:

When my husband and I were newly married, we loved to entertain, but had little money. Our solution was Polenta Parties. I would make a big pot of polenta and some marinara sauce. Each guest would bring something to add to the polenta dish: Italian sausage, tiny meatballs, diced chicken, olives, peppers, onions, tomatoes, mushrooms, at least 3 kinds of cheese -- whatever! The marinara sauce would be poured over the polenta topped with all the contributions on a large platter. Everyone would gather around equipped with a napkin, and the party would begin!

POLENTA PUDDING

1 recipe of Polenta (see page 54)
½ lb. Mozzarella cheese, thinly
   sliced
White pepper, to taste
3 Tbsps. butter

Make polenta and pour into a 14''x 9'' pan about ½'' deep. Spread evenly and chill. Cut the chilled polenta to fit a bread pan greased with 1 tablespoon of the butter. Insert a layer of polenta, cover with slices of cheese and a little pepper. Continue to layer until all ingredients are used -- finishing with polenta as the top layer. Dot with remaining 2 tablespoons of the butter and bake in a very hot oven (450°) until top is browned, 20-25 minutes. Serve hot or cold. Serves 4.

MANICOTTI

Manicotti is a tube pasta approximately 4'' long and 1'' in diameter. It is always stuffed. This filling is particularly delicious.

Pasta:

2 cups meat sauce (see page 61)
12 manicotti cases, uncooked

Filling:

1 lb. Ricotta cheese
1 large egg, well beaten
1 Tbsp. parsley, finely minced
½ cup Parmesan cheese, grated
½ tsp. dry basil
½ tsp. nutmeg
Salt and pepper to taste

Place all filling ingredients in a large bowl and using a wire whisk, blend until smooth.
Cover the bottom of a two quart baking dish with 1 cup of the meat sauce. Fill uncooked manicotti cases with filling, using a small spoon or pastry bag, and arrange in single layer in the dish. Cover with the rest of meat sauce. Cover the top of baking dish with foil and bake for 1 hour in a 375° oven. Serves 6.

MAMA'S NOODLE RING

Notes from Patti:

It has been said that when Thomas Jefferson visited Italy, he so loved pasta he ordered the first pasta machine to be brought to our country.

½ lb. egg noodles, cooked al
    dente and drained
¼ cup (½ cube) butter, melted
2 eggs, lightly beaten
½ cup milk
3 Tbsps. Dry Sherry
1 cup cheddar cheese, coarsely
    grated
Salt and pepper, to taste
Butter to coat mold
½ cup dry bread crumbs

Butter a 1½ quart ring mold and coat with bread crumbs. Mix noodles with butter, eggs, milk, Dry Sherry, cheddar cheese and salt and pepper. Pour into mold. Place mold in a pan half filled with hot water. Bake in a 350° oven, uncovered 30-40 minutes. Unmold on a warm platter. Serves 4.

FARFALLA AND ITALIAN SAUSAGE

6 Tbsps. olive oil
1 medium onion, coarsely
    chopped
1 large stalk celery, coarsely
    chopped
3 small Italian sausage, peeled
    and finely chopped
1 cup Chardonnay*
2 cups canned mushroom sauce
1 lb. Farfalla (pasta shaped like
    little bows)
¾ cup Parmesan Cheese, freshly
    grated

Heat olive oil in a large skillet until haze forms. Add onion and celery and cook until onion is transparent. Add sausage and cook until lightly browned. Add Chardonnay and cook until wine has been reduced to half. Add mushroom sauce, reduce heat and simmer 25 minutes, stirring often.

Cook Farfalla in 6 quarts of boiling salted water until al dente. Drain in large colander and transfer to heated platter. Cover with sauce and mix until pasta is well coated. Add Parmesan cheese and mix well. Serves 6.

    * A dry French Colombard may be substituted for the Chardonnay.

VERMICELLI AND ZINFANDEL

¾ cup vermicelli, broken in
   small pieces
4 cups beef stock
1 cup Zinfandel*
1 tsp. red wine vinegar
1 tsp. lemon juice

Garnish:

1½ Tbsps. chopped chives

Cook vermicelli in lots of boiling salted water, 6 to 8 minutes. Drain. Pour stock, Zinfandel, vinegar, lemon juice into a large pot; bring to simmer and add vermicelli. Simmer until vermicelli is hot. Sprinkle chives as garnish. Serves 6.

   *Barbera may be substituted for Zinfandel.

Notes from Patti:

Vermicelli is a type of spaghetti used in Naples and the regions of southern Italy. It is almost twice as thin as spaghetti and somewhat longer in length. Neopolitians swear it is much easier to twirl on a fork.

LOTS OF CHEESE LASAGNE

1 8 oz. package cream cheese, at
   room temperature
1 pint sour cream, at room
   temperature
1 pint ricotta cheese, at room
   temperature
1 large onion, finely minced
½ lb. lasagne noodles
2-3 cups meat sauce (see page 61)

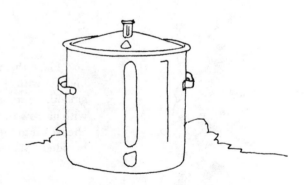

Blend the sour cream and the cheeses together. Fold in the onion. Cover and refrigerate for 24 hours. Bring to room temperature before using.

Cook lasagne in a large 8 quart pot of salted boiling water until al dente. Pour several cups of cold water into the pot and drain thoroughly. Spread pasta on paper toweling and pat dry. In a 14''x 9'' pan place a layer of lasagne pasta lengthwise and spread a thick layer of cheese sauce. Place the next layer of lasagne pasta crosswise (cut with kitchen shears and/or use the shorter, broken pieces to form layer). Add another layer of cheese sauce. Continue layers, ending with lasagne pasta. Cover with meat sauce. Cover pan with foil and bake ½ hour in 350° oven. Serves 8.

Notes from Patti:

Always use the lattice method of layering Lasagne. This prevents it from falling apart when served.

PESTO

I am convinced there is no such thing as an "authentic" pesto recipe, since the ingredients vary so greatly. The only consistent ingredients are basil and garlic. I find good pesto is like good wine, one becomes addicted. Since the basil season is short, about 3 months, I always make large quantities, omitting cheese, butter and pasta water, and freeze for future use. After frozen pesto is thawed, add the cheeses, butter and pasta water. Don't limit pesto to just pasta. It is wonderful for fish and meat and in soups and sauces.

Notes from Patti:

This is a natural for the food processor. Use a chopping blade and add all ingredients. Blend until you have a smooth sauce.

*2 cups tightly packed basil leaves
(must be fresh!)*
½ cup olive oil
*2 large cloves garlic, finely
minced*
2 Tbsps. pine nuts
1 tsp. salt
*2 Tbsps. pasta water (water that
pasta has been cooked in)*
*½ cup Parmesan cheese, freshly
grated*
*3 Tbsps. Romano cheese, freshly
grated*
*3 Tbsps. butter (must be butter,
at room temperature)*

Place the basil, which has been stemmed and torn into small pieces, into blender with olive oil, garlic, pine nuts and salt. Blend on high speed until very smooth (stop occasionally and push ingredients to the bottom of the container with narrow rubber spatula). Pour into a bowl and beat the pasta water and the cheeses into the mixture, using a wire whip. Add the butter and beat until well blended. Makes 1½ cups.

GARLIC SAUCE

5 cloves of garlic, finely minced
2 large eggs plus 1 egg yolk
½ tsp. salt
2 cups olive oil

Combine garlic, eggs and egg yolk, salt and ¼ cup of the olive oil in a blender or food processor fitted with a chopping blade and blend about 10 seconds. Add remaining oil a little at a time, as you would for mayonnaise. Serve over pasta. Makes 2½ cups.

MARINARA SAUCE

4 Tbsps. butter
2 Tbsps. olive oil
2 medium onions, coarsely
    chopped
¾ cup carrots, coarsely grated
3 cloves garlic, finely minced
4 cups canned Italian plum
    tomatoes
Salt and pepper, to taste
1 tsp. oregano
1 Tbsps. fresh basil (must be
    fresh)
½ cup Barbera*

In a large skillet heat 2 tablespoons of the butter and the olive oil until a slight haze forms. Add onions, carrots and garlic and sauté until onions are nicely browned. Purée tomatoes in a blender and add to vegetables. Season with salt and pepper. Partially cover and simmer on low heat 15 minutes. Cool slightly. Pour into blender and puree until very smooth (vegetables will not be visible). Return purée to skillet and add final 2 tablespoons butter, oregano, basil, Barbera and salt and pepper to taste. Cook on low heat, partially covered, an additional ½ hour. Makes 1 quart.
*Pinot Noir may be substituted for the Barbera.

Notes from Patti:

My friend, Maria, who was born of the East Coast, tells of helping her mother cook for Italian men who immigrated to America without their families. Many of these men, unable to speak English and unaccustomed to wild game and strange tasting vegetables, sought out Italian families for room and board. It was not unusual to have 15 to 20 men at the dinner table. Many Italian women turned their living rooms into restaurants, as did Maria's mother. It wasn't long before their food became popular with non-Italians, too. It became a pastime to "eat with the Italians" and drink their "red ink", the nickname given to Chianti. Today there is no region of the country that doesn't boast of an Italian restaurant.

CROCKPOT SPAGHETTI SAUCE
(Great Aunt Mary's Woodstove Sauce)

Notes from Patti:

The flavor of this sauce is quite pungent and compliments a wide variety of foods. As a pasta sauce I add ½ pound fresh mushrooms, cut in thick slices, the last 20 minutes of cooking. Try a little of the sauce over freshly cooked green beans. Great for Eggplant Parmesan. Bake fish in it. Brown cut up chicken, transfer to a large casserole, cover with the sauce and bake, covered, in a 350° oven for 30 minutes.

I've had some really fine female role models in my life and my great Aunt Mary was one of the best. She was a strong woman, physically, mentally and spiritually, and the best story teller I've ever heard. No matter what work we were doing, from weeding the garden to canning and preserving its bounty, she made the hours fly by with her wonderful tales. For Aunt Mary there were no grey areas in life, only right and wrong and that is the way she lived her 92 years. She never criticized and always encouraged any endeavor we undertook.

1 lb. very lean bacon, cut in 1''
* squares*
3 Tbsps. bacon fat
2 large onions, coarsely chopped
4 cloves garlic, peeled and
* coarsely chopped*
1 28 oz. can stewed tomatoes
4 8 oz. cans tomato sauce
1 cup Zinfandel*
Freshly ground pepper, to taste

Fry bacon until nicely browned. Transfer to paper towels and reserve. Pour off all bacon fat except 3 tablespoons. Sauté onions and garlic in bacon fat until onions are transparent. Transfer to crockpot, add bacon and all remaining ingredients and stir well. Cover and turn to low setting. Cook 12 hours. Makes about 2 quarts.

*Pinot Noir may be substituted for the Zinfandel.

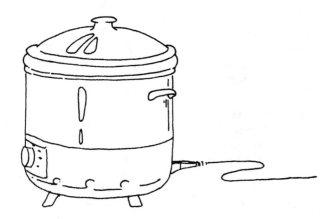

MY FAVORITE MEAT SAUCE

*½ lb. smoked ham, coarsely
   chopped
1 large onion, coarsely chopped
1 large carrot, coarsely shredded
2 Tbsps. butter
1½ lbs. top round steak, ground
   twice
½ lb. lean pork, ground twice
2 Tbsps. olive oil
2 1 lb. cans Italian plum tomatoes, puréed with juice
2 cloves garlic, finely minced
1 cup Barbera*
Salt and pepper, to taste*

Melt the butter in a large skillet and add the ham, onion and carrot. Cook over medium heat, stirring often, until onion is golden (about 10 minutes). Transfer to a large dutch oven (6 quart size).

Heat olive oil in same skillet until a slight haze forms. Add ground round and ground pork and cook until lightly browned. Transfer to dutch oven with the ham, onion, and carrot mixture. Add puréed tomatoes, garlic, Barbera and stir thoroughly. Bring to a boil over high heat, reduce the heat and simmer, partially covered, 45-50 minutes. Salt and pepper to taste. Makes app. 2½ qts.

*Petite Sirah may be substituted for the Barbera.

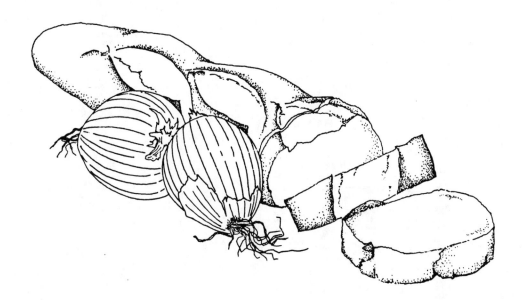

61

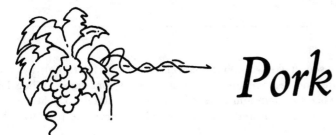

Pork

Although Pappa didn't raise meat and poultry, we had a neighbor who did, and Pappa always helped out during slaughter time. The neighbor, in turn, always gave us a pig and let Pappa use his smokehouse for the task of smoking the bacon, ham and sausages. We also enjoyed the head cheese, crackling (made from the skin) and those delectable pigs feet. Pappa always said you could eat everything from the snout to the tail and he was right. Unfortunately, in the United States, many parts of the pig are discarded: The brains, ears, tongue and tail being the most overlooked. One of the foods I miss the most are those delicious thick slices of home smoked bacon.

Today's packaged bacon is so thin it seems to disappear before your very eyes! I often order a slab of bacon from my butcher instead and slice it myself to the desired thickness. A slab will range in weight from 6 to 10 pounds and keeps well for many weeks in the refrigerator since it is slowly cured (packaged bacon is always quickly cured and only lightly smoked.) I don't advise freezing bacon. All forms of pork should always be well cooked—never pink. With that in mind, enjoy the old-fashioned goodness of pork for a pleasurable change!

HAM A LA BALLARD

This ham may sound like work, but it is well worth the effort. I always make this the day before and remove the fruit to a covered container. When I am ready to serve, I slice the ham and reheat it just long enough to heat through. Put the fruit in a chafing dish and heat thoroughly. Serve the fruit over ham slices.

Ham and Filling:

*1 6-8 lb. FRESH picnic ham
    (must be fresh, a cured ham
    will destroy the flavor of the
    fruit)*
*1 cup pineapple chunks, fresh if
    possible*
*2 firm bananas, cut in large
    chunks*
*1 large peach, peeled, seeded
    and coarsely chopped*
*1 large nectarine, seeded and
    coarsely chopped*
*6 apricots, seeded and coarsely
    chopped*
*6 plums, seeded and coarsely
    chopped*
1 cup Plum Wine

Basting Sauce:

*½ cup dark brown sugar, firmly
    packed*
1 cup Plum Wine

Have your butcher bone the fresh ham and cut a 2½ to 3 cup cavity in the center of the ham; then have the butcher cut two end pieces of the bones, 3 to 4 inches each.

Plug up one end of ham with the bone and fill the cavity with the fresh fruit. Pour in the Plum Wine and insert the other piece of bone in the opening. Tie a string around the ham to keep the plugs in place. Place the ham on a rack in a shallow roasting pan. Bake in 375° oven 24 minutes per pound. Bast every 25 to 30 minutes until done. Serves 10 to 12.

HAM AND PEPPERS WITH PASTA

Sauce:

2 Tbsps. butter
2 Tbsps. olive oil
3 fresh green onions, including
  the green tops, thinly sliced
½ green pepper, seeded and
  coursely chopped, or ¼ cup
  chopped pimento
6 large fresh mushrooms, thinly
  sliced
¾ cup cooked ham, cut in 1 inch
  strips
½ cup heavy cream

Pasta:

1 batch fresh pasta, cut in thin
  strips (If you must use store
  pasta, get the thin noodles)
3 Tbsps. butter
⅓ cup heavy cream
½ cup Pamesan cheese, freshly
  grated

Melt the 2 tablespoons butter and the olive oil in a large skillet. Sauté onions, peppers, mushrooms and ham until peppers are soft. Add the ½ cup cream and cook until the mixture is slightly thickened.

Cook the pasta quickly, drain and return to pot. Add the 3 tablespoons butter and ⅓ cup cream. Toss until butter is melted. Stir in cheese and toss. Transfer to heated platter and pour the ham and pepper sauce on top. Serve at once. Top each serving with additional cheese. Serves 4.

MARINATED PORK CHOPS

6 pork chops, about ¾ inch thick
2 cloves garlic, finely minced
3 tsps. paprika
Salt and freshly ground black
  pepper, to taste
1 cup dry French Colombard*

Arrange pork chops in shallow baking dish. Combine garlic, paprika, salt and pepper and sprinkle over pork chops. Add the French Colombard, cover and refrigerate for 6 hours. Leave chops in the marinade and bake in a 300° oven, uncovered, for 1 hour. Serves 6.

*Pinot Blanc may be substituted for French Colombard.

ORANGE MARSALA PORK CHOPS

4 double thick cut loin pork chops
2 cups cornbread stuffing mix
3 Tbsps. butter, melted
½ tsp. salt
⅓ cup orange juice
Salt and pepper, to taste
½ cup Orange Marsala*
1 tsp. orange peel, grated

Cut a horizontal slit in the side of each chop, forming a pocket for stuffing.
Combine stuffing mix with butter, salt and orange juice. Fill pockets with stuffing and secure with toothpicks. Salt and pepper both sides. Place in shallow baking dish.
Mix Orange Marsala with orange peel. Brush the chops with ½ of the sauce; cover with foil. Place in a 350° oven for ½ hour. Uncover and baste with remaining sauce. Continue to bake, uncovered, an additional ½ hour. Serves 4.
*Orange liqueur may be substituted for Orange Marsala.

APRICOT PORK ROAST

1 4 lb. pork loin roast
6 strips bacon, coarsely chopped
1 bay leaf
2 cloves
1 sprig of fresh thyme
1 cup Apricot Wine*
Salt and pepper, to taste

Cook bacon in a large Dutch Oven until crisp. Leave bacon and remove all but 2 tablespoons of the fat. Add roast and brown on all sides. Sprinkle with salt and pepper and add all remaining ingredients. Bring to a boil, cover, reduce heat and simmer for 2½ hours. Remove roast to a large platter and slice. Discard the bay leaf, cloves and thyme. Pour the liquid over the sliced roast and serve. Serves 6.
*There is no substitute for Apricot Wine.

AUNT MARY'S PORK PIE

Filling:

3 lbs. very lean pork, cut in ½"
   cubes
2 small white onions, coarsely
   chopped
2 cloves garlic, finely minced
4 cooking apples, peeled, cored
   and coarsely chopped
2 tsps. mace
¼ cup Dry Sherry
2 tsps. salt
1 tsp. pepper
3 medium eggs, beaten
2½ cups fresh bread crumbs

Meat Pie Crust:

1½ cups all purpose flour
½ cup cake flour (fine pastry
   flour)
6 Tbsps. lard, frozen and cut into
   6 equal pieces
⅓ cup very cold water
½ tsp. salt

Glaze:

1 egg
½ tsp. salt

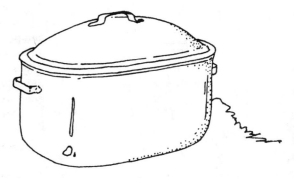

Cook pork in a dutch oven, over medium heat, until any fat has been rendered. Pour off fat. Add onions, garlic, apples, mace, Dry Sherry, salt and pepper. Remove from heat and cool. Add beaten eggs and bread crumbs and stir well. Set aside. Place flours and salt in a large bowl and cut in lard until it is in pea-size pieces. Add water slowly and quickly incorporate until dough is smooth. Or use a food processor, fitted with a chopping blade. Add all ingredients and process, turning on/off 5 to 6 times. Continue processing until ball of dough forms. Chill at least 1 hour before using.

Roll out pastry on lightly floured surface, about ¼ inch thick. Line a 9" springform pan with the pastry, reserving all leftover pastry. Place on cookie sheet. Fill with pork pie mixture. Re-roll extra pastry and place on top of filling. Trim excess with a sharp knife. Crimp edges together. Cut a small round hole in middle of top crust. Cut daisy petals and a stem from any remaining pastry. Place the petals around the hole, add stem. Beat the egg and salt of the glaze together, then brush generously over crust. Bake in preheated 400° oven for 15 minutes. Reduce heat to 325° and bake for 1 hour. Cool slightly and remove from pan. Serves 6.

SWEET AND SOUR SPARERIBS (Crockpot Style)

*5 pounds spareribs, cut in two rib
    pieces
Salt and pepper, to taste
¼ cup pineapple juice
3 Tbsps. red wine vinegar
½ cup Honey Wine*
2 Tbsps. soy sauce
2 Tbsps. honey
2 tsps. arrowroot
3-4 Tbsps. cold water*

Place spareribs on rack in a shallow baking pan. Brown in a 400⁰ oven for 30 minutes, turning once. Remove from oven, pour off fat and sprinkle with salt and pepper. Place ribs in crockpot. Combine all ingredients, except arrowroot and water, and pour over ribs. Cover and cook on low setting 9 to 10 hours. Remove ribs to a warm platter. Turn heat control to high. Dissolve arrowroot in the cold water. Gradually stir into rib cooking liquid. Stir until slightly thickened, 10 to 15 minutes. Pour over spareribs and serve at once. Serves 4.

*Mead Wine or honey liqueur (such as Drambuie) may be substituted for the honey wine.

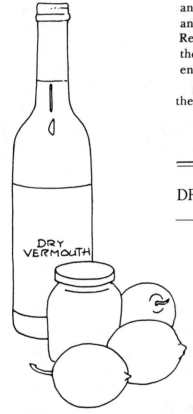

DRY VERMOUTH PORK ROAST

*1 4 lb. pork loin roast
1 cup Dry Vermouth
1 cup water
1 tsp. salt
1 tsp. thyme
1 tsp. rosemary
1 bay leaf
2 cloves garlic, finely chopped
1 Tbsp. grated lemon peel
1 Tbsps. lemon juice*

Remove all visible fat from the roast and place in a large bowl. Combine all remaining ingredients and pour over roast. Cover and refrigerate 10 to 12 hours. Transfer roast to crockpot. Remove bay leaf from marinade and discard. Pour marinade over roast, cover and cook on low for 12 hours. Drain and slice. This roast is also very good served cold with hot mustard and a side dish of coleslaw. Serves 6-8.

PICKLED PIGS' FEET

In another part of this book, I told about the luscious smells and colors of my Grandmother's kitchen, and one of the things that contributed to those smells was the crock of pickled pigs feet she always kept. Her butcher was also her friend, she always brought him her special soups and homemade bread. He would never dream of charging her for soup bones, and even though others paid for pigs feet, Grandmother never did.

Pigs feet:

8 pigs feet, split lengthwise
Cold water
2 stalks of celery, each cut in half
1 large onion, cut in quarters
2 carrots, each cut in half
2 cloves of garlic, peeled and cut
* in half*
1 bay leaf
3 sprigs of parsley
8 peppercorns

Brine
1 large white onion, finely
* chopped*
2 carrots, very thinly sliced
2 cloves garlic, peeled and
* minced*
3 cups cooking liquid
1½ cups red wine vinegar
1 bay leaf
4 peppercorns
4 cloves
½ tsp. marjoram
½ tsp. mace
½ tsp. dill weed
1 Tbsp. sugar

Scrub the pigs feet with a stiff brush. Wrap the feet in cheesecloth and tie the ends. Put the feet in a 6-8 quart pot. Add the remaining ingredients and cover with plenty of cold water. Bring to a rolling boil, reduce heat and simmer 4 to 5 hours or until tender. Drain thoroughly, reserving 3 cups of the cooking liquid. Allow the feet to cool to room temperature.

Unwrap the pigs feet and place in a crock. Sprinkle the onions, carrots and garlic evenly over the top.

Bring the cooking liquid, vinegar, bay leaf, peppercorns, cloves, marjoram, mace, dill and sugar to a rolling boil; reduce heat and simmer about 5 minutes. Remove bay leaf and pour over pigs feet. Refrigerate and let stand 3-4 days before serving.

The leftover cooking liquid is a very good base to cook neck bones or tongue. As for the marinade (brine), just keep adding to it. Once you have tasted these pigs feet, you will never again buy those dull tasting expensive ones on the grocer's shelf. Serves 8.

JERRY PREDIKA'S HOMEMADE ITALIAN SAUSAGE

Jerry Predika, whose grandparents were born in Russia, is a multitalented gentleman. He is a professional artist whose paintings reflect the Russian Byzantine era, and a restorer of Victorian kitchens so beautiful they make you yearn for yesteryear. One of the great eaters and wine drinkers of our time, he is also a sausage maker extraordinaire, with a yet-to-be-published book on the subject (Jerry says his pigs are cleaner than most people!) He is a splendid fellow and once you taste these sausages, you will want to have them on hand all the time! They're especially good with a hot German-style mustard.

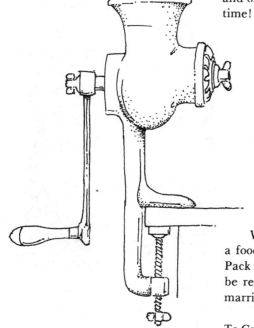

20 lbs. pork butt
5 oz. salt
⅛ cup black pepper, freshly
ground
¼ cup fennel, crushed
½ cup paprika
½ cup dried hot chili peppers*,
crushed

Without removing any fat from pork butt, grind coarsely with a ⅜ blade of a food grinder. Add all remaining ingredients to pork and blend thoroughly. Pack in 2'' x 18'' hog intestines casings and tie off at 6'' lengths. Sausage must be refrigerated for 24 hours before cooking or freezing to allow the complete marriage of flavors.

To Cook:

Place needed number of sausages per serving into an ovenproof casserole, cover, and bake in a 350° oven for 45 minutes.

To Freeze:

Place sausages into plastic bags, seal and place in freezer until needed.
*The dried, hot peppers are the red varietal found in Mexican grocery stores, which also carry a variety of sausage casings.

Notes from Patti:

Jerry tells me you can get a good hand operated grinder with a sausage stuffing attachment for around $20 at popular department stores, but if you know your butcher well, and you should, ask him to grind the pork for you. Buy pork butts when they are on sale and freeze for future use.

JEFF BOOTH'S CHILI VERDE

Jeff Booth is a young California winemaker who started as a part-time winery worker while still in college. Jeff's father, a southern California college professor, was a devotee of the foods and drinks of Mexico and the family spent their summers traveling the whole of that country. Jeff often assisted his father in preparing authentic Mexican dishes for family and friends and quickly developed his own skills in the kitchen.

3 pounds pork shoulder, cut into
*   1 inch cubes*
1 large onion, coarsely chopped
5 cloves garlic, coarsely chopped
3 Tbsps. olive oil
2 12 oz. cans tomatillos (green
*   tomatoes) cut in fourths*
4 7 oz. cans green chilis, seeded
*   and cut into strips*
½ tsp. cumin
½ tsp. coriander seeds
4 beef bouillon cubes, dissolved
*   in ¼ cup boiling water*
4-5 grinds black pepper, freshly
*   ground*
¾ cup Barbera*

Brown pork cubes in a large dutch oven. Remove and set aside. Pour off any remaining fat. Add olive oil and sauté onions and garlic until the onions are limp. Return the pork cubes to the pan. Add tomatillos, green chilis, cumin, coriander, oregano, the dissolved bouillon cubes, pepper and the Barbera. Bring to a boil, reduce heat, cover and simmer 2 hours. Remove cover and simmer an additional 45 minutes or until the sauce is reduced to the thickness you want. Serve over rice. Serves 8.

*Pinot Noir may be substituted for the Barbera.

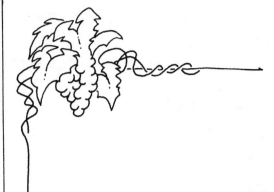

Poultry

Just as Grandma always grew her own vegetables, she also raised her own poultry, both for the meat and the eggs. Although she kept a few ducks and turkeys, she always said the chicken was the noblest bird of them all. As a child, I remember watching Grandma choose her bird for whatever dish she had in mind. If she was going to stuff the bird and roast it to a deep golden hue, it had to have an amply plump breast. If she had chicken soup or chicken and pasta dumplings in mind, then her choice was the older hen that wasn't laying eggs and took a longer time to cook. She taught me the versatility of the noble bird -- that you can do anything from elegant stuffed breast to a simple and delicious broiled chicken with dry Vermouth and lemon juice. Today's chickens live an austere dormitory life which eliminates some of their character. Nevertheless the chicken remains one of our best buys and most delicious foods.

BAKED SHERRY CHICKEN

Notes from Patti:

If you don't know how to cut up a whole chicken or bone a chicken breast, you should learn. If you compare the price of whole chickens on sale to cut up chicken on sale, you will find quite a difference.

At the risk of repeating myself, this recipe is easy, easy easy, easy! It takes less than 5 minutes to put together.

> *2 frying chickens, each cut in*
> *half*
> *½ cup olive oil*
> *4 Tbsps. butter*
> *¾ cup Dry Sherry*
> *1½ tsps. mixed Italian herbs*
> *(any commercial brand)*
> *1 tsp. paprika (I like more)*
> *½ lb. medium size mushrooms*

Pour oil in large baking pan. Arrange chicken skin side up. Dot with butter and sprinkle with seasonings. Pour Dry Sherry over chicken. Cover. Bake in 325° oven for 45 minutes. Baste two to three times. Add whole mushrooms and bake 15 additional minutes. Serves 4.

CHICKEN AND ARTICHOKE HEARTS

This is a great party dish since it can be made the day before and reheated just before serving.

> *1 3 to 4 lb. chicken, cut up*
> *¾ cup flour*
> *1 tsp. salt*
> *½ cup corn oil*
> *1 9 oz. package artichoke hearts*
> *2 cups Crockpot Spaghetti Sauce*
> *(see page 60)*

Place flour and salt in a paper bag and shake to mix. Add a few pieces of chicken at a time and shake to coat. Heat oil in a large skillet and brown chicken to a golden brown. Place frozen artichoke hearts in an ovenproof casserole. Arrange browned chicken pieces on top of artichokes. Pour the spaghetti sauce over chicken, cover and bake in a 350° oven for 45 minutes. Serves 6.

CHICKEN AND RICE

Chicken:

2 3 lb. chickens
2 celery stalks, thickly sliced
2 small onions, thickly sliced
2 large carrots, cut into fourths
¾ cup Pinot Blanc*
3 tsps. salt
1 clove
6 peppercorns

Rice:

1 small onion, finely chopped
2-3 Tbsps. butter
2 cups uncooked rice
3 cups broth from chicken

Sauce:

3 cups broth from chicken
2 Tbsps. arrowroot
Salt and pepper to taste

   Place chickens in large pot with celery, onions, carrots, Pinot Blanc, salt, clove and peppercorns. Cover with cool water (about 3 quarts). Bring to a boil; skim off any foam. Cover and simmer on low heat about 1½ hours.
   One half hour before chicken is done sauté onion in 2-3 tablespoons butter. Add rice and 1 cup of the broth from the chicken. As rice soaks up broth, slowly add more broth until rice is done (about 3 cups total). Place rice in a ring on a warm platter. Remove chicken from broth. Slip chicken from bones and place in center of ring of rice.
   Place 3 cups of the remaining broth in large sauce pan. Dissolve arrowroot in ¼ cup water. Add to broth on low heat and stir until thickened. Season with salt and pepper to taste. Pour over chicken and rice. Serves 8.
   *Chardonnay may be substituted for the Pinot Blanc.

CHICKEN BARBERA

I've already mentioned the importance of using good wine for cooking. Very few recipes use as much wine as this chicken dish, but, when called for, it is essential to use only the very best. This is a great party dish, since everything is done 24 hours in advance of cooking. Just put the chicken in the oven. Then pour yourself a glass of ice cold champagne to sip while you change into your best bib "n" tucker and have a wonderful time!

Chicken:

2 large fryers, cut into pieces,
*   move all visible fat from cavities*
1 4/5 qt. bottle Barbera*

Marinade:

2 large onions, coarsely chopped
⅓ cup olive oil
½ cup red wine vinegar
2 bay leaves
1 tsp. thyme
1 tsp. oregano
½ tsp. rosemary
½ tsp. dill weed
4 large cloves garlic, finely minced

Sauce:

4 strips lean bacon cut into 1" pieces
1 large bunch fresh green onions,
*   including green tops, finely chopped*
2 large carrots, coarsely grated
2 8 oz. cans tomato sauce

Place chicken in a large dutch oven. Combine all marinade ingredients. Pour over chicken and mix well. Cover and marinate in refrigerator for 24 hours.

Make sauce. Fry bacon in a large skillet. Remove from skillet and reserve. Discard all but 1 tablespoon bacon fat. Add onions and carrots and sauté until carrots are wilted. Add reserved bacon and tomato sauce. Cook on low heat for 10 minutes. Refrigerate for 24 hours.

Bring chicken and marinade to room temperature, remove bay leaves and discard.

Add sauce to marinated chicken. *DO NOT REMOVE MARINADE.* Mix well. Pour 1 six ounce glass of Barbera for you and pour the rest of the wine into the chicken. Mix well, cover and bake in a 300° oven for 1½ hours. Serve with lots of sourdough bread to sop up the fabulous sauce. Serves 10 hearty eaters.

*This recipe was specifically designed for the flavor of a great California Barbera. Therefore, I offer no substitute.

CABERNET AND DRY SHERRY CHICKEN

2 Tbsps. butter
2 Tbsps. olive oil
1 3 lb. chicken, cut up
Liver, heart and gizzard, very
    finely chopped
1 small bunch green onions,
    including green tops, finely
    chopped
2 cloves garlic, finely chopped
4 sprigs parsley, finely chopped
3-4 Tbsps. flour
1 tsp. brown mustard
2 cups beef broth
1 cup Cabernet Sauvignon*
¼ tsp. thyme
¼ tsp. rosemary
½ tsp. paprika
¼ cup Dry Sherry

Heat butter and oil in heavy skillet. Sauté chicken until nicely browned; remove. Add liver, heart, gizzard, green onions, garlic and parsley. Cook until tender and remove from pan. Blend flour into drippings, add mustard, beef broth and Cabernet Sauvignon. Cook, stirring constantly until smooth and slightly thickened. Add thyme, rosemary, paprika. Salt and pepper to taste. Return chicken to sauce. Add liver mixture. Cover and simmer on low flame until done - about ½ hour. Add Sherry. Simmer 10 minutes more. Serves 4.

*Zinfandel may be substituted for the Cabernet Sauvignon

GRANDMA'S CHICKEN AND PASTA

I can't remember a time when our family didn't cook this dish. It was one of my father's favorites and, as a child, I often asked Grandma to make it.

3 medium size chicken breast
halves, skinned, boned and
cut into thin strips
3 Tbsps. butter
1 Tbsp. olive oil
1 large clove garlic, finely
chopped
1 small bunch green onions,
including green tops, finely
chopped
½ cup Dry Vermouth
1 Tbsp. flour
⅓ cup heavy cream
½ cup Gruyere cheese, freshly
grated
½ cup Parmesan cheese, freshly
grated
½ tsp. salt
Freshly ground black pepper,
to taste
2 Tbsps. parsley, finely chopped
1 lb. homemade noodles
(see page 52)

Heat butter and oil in a heavy skillet. Add chicken strips and cook until firm, stirring constantly (about 4 to 5 minutes). Add garlic and green onions and continue to cook for 2 to 3 minutes more. Add Dry Vermouth and cook one more minute. Stir in flour and cook until smooth. Add cream, cheeses and parsley and cook until the cheeses have melted.

Cook noodles according to directions and drain. Toss with chicken and sauce and serve immediately. Serves 4.

TANGY CHICKEN SALAD

Salad:

3 cups cooked chicken, diced
1 cup celery, thinly sliced
3 Tbsps. pimento, diced
1½ tsps. candied (crystallized)
   ginger, chopped
½ cup toasted almonds, slivered
½ cup sour cream
¼ cup mayonnaise
1 Tbsp. red wine vinegar

To Serve:

6 slices pineapple, chilled
6 large lettuce leaves
6 tiny cherry tomatoes

Notes from Patti:

Cooked, diced chicken in your freezer will allow you to whip up elegant dishes, like this great old-fashioned chicken salad, in a matter of minutes.

Combine chicken, celery, pimento, ginger and almonds. Mix sour cream, mayonnaise and vinegar until smooth. Pour over chicken and mix thoroughly. Chill.

Place chilled pineapple slices on lettuce leaf. Heap chicken salad on pineapple. Garnish with sprig of fresh parsley and a tiny cherry tomato. Serves 6.

ALMOND MARSALA CHICKEN CASSEROLE

3 cups cooked chicken, cut in bite
   size pieces
2 cups celery, coarsely chopped
¾ cup green onions, coarsely
   chopped
¼ cup Almond Marsala
⅓ cup lemon juice
1 can cream of chicken soup
⅔ cups Pinot Blanc*
2 cups cooked rice
⅔ cup bread crumbs

Notes from Patti:

Marsala takes its name from the city of Marsala in western Sicily and is the best known of Italian fortified wines. There are many kinds of Marsalas, ranging from the sweet through medium to very dry (fine) Marsalas. Sweet Marsala is served as a liqueur while the dry Marsala is a wonderfully different apertif.

Combine chicken, celery, green onions, Almond Marsala and lemon juice. Dilute cream of chicken soup with the Pinot Blanc. Blend into mixture. Fold in rice. Pour into a 2 quart buttered mold or baking dish, top with bread crumbs and bake in a 350° oven for 1 hour. Serves 4.

*Fume Blanc may be substituted for the Pinot Blanc.

STUFFED CHICKEN BREAST

February 27, 1981

Patricia Ballard
Bargetto Winery
3535 North Main Street
Soquel, California 95073

Dear Patti:

Fine wine and charming guests can only enhance the Epicurean delights you prepare.

Since my profession is one in which tastes dictate production, I can certainly appreciated the efforts required in preparing a superb dinner party.

Of the many dishes you prepared on that memorable evening at your home, your Stuffed Chicken Breast deserves special mention. The taste of chicken breasts stuffed with prosciutto and mozzarella cheese served in a wine and mushroom sauce was extremely delightful. All I can say is it was marvelous and inimitable.

Thank you so much for a superb evening and a delicious dinner.

Gratefully,

Lawrence Bargetto
President / Winemaster

Notes from Patti:

Commercially made bread crumbs are not inexpensive -- about 80¢ for 9 ounces. Save leftover bread, dry it in your oven (a convection oven is perfect for this use), throw it in your blender or food processor fitted with a chopping blade, add your own choice of herbs and seasonings and process as coarse or fine as you like.

These chicken breasts look small, but they plump to almost double in size when cooked.

> 4 whole chicken breasts, skin-
>   ned, boned and cut in half lengthwise
> 8 thin slices Prosciutto (Italian ham)
> 8 thin slices Mozzarella cheese
> 1 tsp. salt
> 2 eggs, well beaten
> 1½ to 2 cups seasoned bread crumbs
> 3 Tbsps. olive oil
> 2 Tbsps. butter
> ¾ cup Chardonnay*
> ½ lb. mushrooms, thickly sliced

Place chicken breasts between waxed paper and pound, with a wooden mallet, to ½'' thickness. Place 1 slice of Prosciutto and 1 slice of Mozzarella on each chicken breast. Roll up and secure with 1 or 2 toothpicks. Blend 1 teaspoon salt into eggs. Dip chicken into egg, roll in seasoned bread crumbs until well coated. Chill ½ hour.

Heat olive oil and butter in a large skillet over low heat. Add chicken breasts, being careful not to crowd, and brown about 1 minute on each side. Transfer to serving platter and keep warm. Add Chardonnay to pan juices; simmer 2 to 3 minutes until alcohol has burned off. Add mushrooms and continue to simmer until mushrooms are tender -- about 5 minutes. Pour sauce over chicken breast and serve immediately. Serves 8.

*Pinot Blanc may be substituted for Chardonnay.

TURKEY WITH APRICOT DRESSING

This is a wonderful holiday bird, but the subtle flavoring of apricots, walnuts and cornbread always makes one think of Springtime. So don't limit this delicious fellow to holidays and please don't discard the turkey carcass. It makes wonderful turkey soup

Turkey:

1 15-20 lb. turkey
1 Tbsp. salt
1 4/5 qt. bottle Apricot Wine

Dressing:

¾ lb dried apricots, cut in
*   quarters*
1 loaf stale sour French bread,
*   torn into bite size pieces*
1 8''x 10'' baking pan of stale
*   cornbread, coarsely crumbled*
1 large onion, coarsely chopped
2 cups celery, finely chopped
4 large cloves garlic, finely
*   minced*
¼ cup parsley, coarsely chopped
1 cup walnuts, coarsely chopped
2 Tbsps. dry mustard
1 tsp. rosemary
1 tsp. dill weed
1 tsp. thyme
Salt and pepper to taste

Sauce:

1 Tbsp. arrowroot
2 cups cream

Marinate dried apricots in enough Apricot Wine to cover. Refrigerate for 24 hours. Drain and reserve the wine. Toss together the dressing ingredients in a large mixing bowl. Add the reserved Apricot Wine and toss lightly. If dressing is too dry, add a little more wine. Rub the turkey cavity with 1 tablespoon of salt, Stuff the wishbone cavity loosely and skewer the skin to the back. Shape the wings akimbo, bringing tips onto the back of wings. Stuff the main cavity loosely (do not pack tightly -- dressing expands during roasting). Close the cavity with skewers and lace it closed with cord. Place the turkey, breast side up, in a V rack in a large roasting pan. Pour the remaining wine into the pan. Baste the turkey thoroughly. Soak a double thickness of cheesecloth in the wine and cover the bird. Baste every ½ hour. Bake at 325° allowing 18 to 20 minutes per pound. Remove the cheesecloth the last ½ hour and baste again. Remove to a warm platter and let the bird rest 15 to 20 minutes.

Place baking pan on top of stove over low heat. Loosen any bits stuck to the pan. Add 1 tablespoon arrowroot and blend in. Add cream (half and half won't do). Stir until sauce is thick enough to coat a wooden spoon. Add a dash of salt and white pepper. Serve at once. Serves 12.

Notes from Patti:

This recipe also works well with cornish game hens. Make ¼ of the dressing recipe for 6 medium size hens. Bake for 1 hour at 350°, basting frequently with the wine.

CHICKEN MARSALA WITH MUSHROOM SAUCE

Notes from Patti:

You may use a *good* vin ordinaire (jug wine), in this recipe. Once again I emphasize the importance of good wine; but there is nothing wrong with drinking or cooking with jug wines you enjoy. I do it all the time!

Chicken:

3 whole chicken breasts skinned,
* boned and cut into ½" strips*
1 large egg
½ tsp. salt
1 cup seasoned bread crumbs
2 Tbsps. olive oil
1 Tbsp. butter

Sauce:

2½ cups dry Chenin Blanc*
½ cup Dry Marsala
3 Tbsps. lemon juice
1 Tbsp. arrowroot
1 lb. mushrooms, thickly sliced
Freshly ground pepper, to taste

Beat egg and salt together. Dip chicken strips in egg and roll in seasoned bread crumbs until well coated. Pour olive oil and butter in a large skillet. Heat until a light haze forms; add chicken, being careful not to crowd, and brown about 1 minute on each side. Remove, with tongs, to a warm platter, retaining pan juices.

Add dry Chenin Blanc to pan juices and bring to a rolling boil. Lower heat and simmer until wine is reduced to half. Add dry Marsala, lemon juice and mushrooms. Simmer 2 to 3 more minutes. Add arrowroot and simmer until sauce is slightly thick. Stir in pepper and pour over chicken strips. Serve at once. Serves 4.

*A dry Riesling may be substituted for the Chenin Blanc.

EASY TARRAGON CHICKEN BREAST

This is the perfect recipe when you decide to invite guests on the spur of the moment. You have plenty of time to prepare a salad and a vegetable while the chicken simmers.

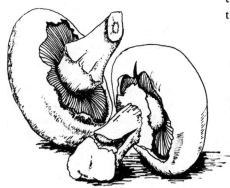

4 chicken breast halves, skinned
* and boned*
¾ lb. mushrooms, thickly sliced
3 Tbsps. butter
1 Tbsp. olive oil
1 cup French Colombard*
½ tsp. tarragon
2 tsp. salt
1 Tbsp. arrowroot

Flatten chicken breasts to half the original thickness with a mallet. Melt butter with the olive oil in a large skillet. Sauté chicken on both sides until light golden brown. Add mushrooms and saute until tneder. Add ¾ cup of the French Colombard, tarragon and salt. Reduce heat to low and simmer, covered, 15 - 20 minutes. Blend the arrowroot into remaining ¼ cup French Colombard. Add to the chicken and stir until sauce thickens. Serve immediately. Serves 4.

*Pinot Blanc may be substituted for the French Colombard.

RENAISSANCE DUCKLING

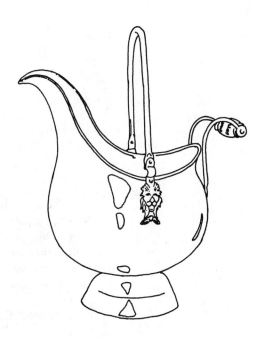

Duck:

1 4-5 lb. duck

Dressing:

3 Tbsps. butter
1 cup walnuts, chopped
1 large onion, finely chopped
4 cups bread crumbs
Grated rind of one lemon
½ tsp. cinnamon
1 tsp. sage
½ tsp. salt
¼ tsp. white pepper
2 eggs, lightly beaten

Glaze:

3 Tbsps. melted butter
⅔ cup Honey Wine*

Melt butter in skillet, add nuts and cook over medium heat until they're browned. Add onions and cook until soft. Remove from heat and stir in remaining ingredients. Stuff cavity of the duck and secure with poultry lacers. Place the duck breast side up on rack in roasting pan. Prick the skin with fork.

Prepare glaze: melt butter, being careful not to brown, then add Honey Wine. Baste the duck generously. Bake in preheated 350° oven 1½ hours. Baste several more times. Serves 6.

*Mead Wine or honey liqueur (such as Drambui) may be substituted for Honey Wine.

DELECTABLE CHICKEN LIVERS

A lot of people don't like livers of any kind, because, like fish, the tendency is to overcook. Freshness is another factor. If you find small greenish spots on liver, it is old and should be discarded. Give this recipe a try - I'm sure you'll love it!

6 Tbsps. butter (only butter will
  do)
1 lb. fresh chicken livers,
  trimmed of any fat
1 lb. mushrooms, thinly sliced
1 small bunch green onions,
  including green tops, thinly
  sliced
1 tsp. salt
1 cup Pinot Blanc*
1 large clove garlic, mashed
¼ tsp. dill weed (I like more)
½ tsp. dry mustard

Melt the butter in a heavy skillet on low heat. Add mushrooms, green onions, garlic and salt. Sauté 5 minutes, until onions are transparent. Push vegetables to the side of the skillet. Add chicken livers and cook only until the edges turn white. Turn livers over, using tongs. Add Pinot Blanc, rosemary, dill weed and mustard and stir well. Simmer on very low heat, uncovered for 8-10 minutes. Serve over homemade egg noodles or rice with the yummy sauce. Serves 4.
*French Colombard may be substituted for Pinot Blanc.

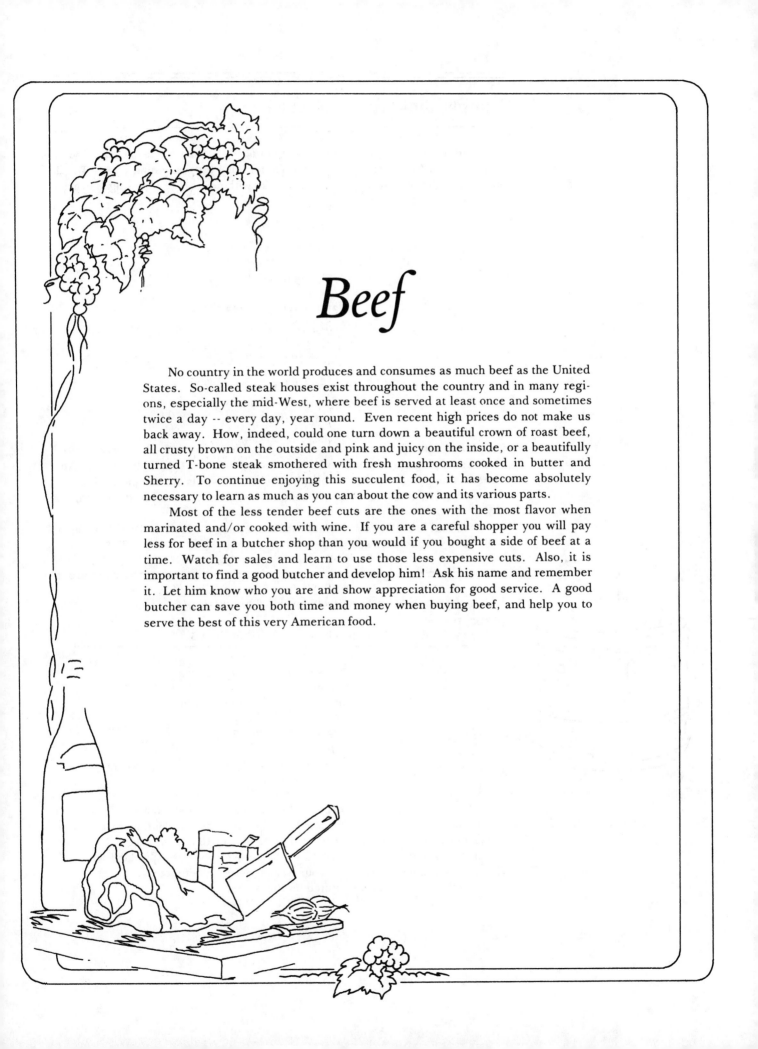

Beef

No country in the world produces and consumes as much beef as the United States. So-called steak houses exist throughout the country and in many regions, especially the mid-West, where beef is served at least once and sometimes twice a day -- every day, year round. Even recent high prices do not make us back away. How, indeed, could one turn down a beautiful crown of roast beef, all crusty brown on the outside and pink and juicy on the inside, or a beautifully turned T-bone steak smothered with fresh mushrooms cooked in butter and Sherry. To continue enjoying this succulent food, it has become absolutely necessary to learn as much as you can about the cow and its various parts.

Most of the less tender beef cuts are the ones with the most flavor when marinated and/or cooked with wine. If you are a careful shopper you will pay less for beef in a butcher shop than you would if you bought a side of beef at a time. Watch for sales and learn to use those less expensive cuts. Also, it is important to find a good butcher and develop him! Ask his name and remember it. Let him know who you are and show appreciation for good service. A good butcher can save you both time and money when buying beef, and help you to serve the best of this very American food.

"MAGIC" SAUCE

This recipe was given to me by a young man from Santa Barbara (Peter Carafiol) and I must say it sounded terrible, but I'll try anything once. Thank goodness I did, because today I wouldn't be without it! The following is exactly the way he gave it to me.

1 cup Tamari *
¼ cup olive oil
¼ cup red wine vinegar
Sesame seeds (lots)
2 large cloves garlic
½ large onion, coarsely chopped
Fresh parsley, to taste
Basil, to taste
Honey, dollop or two - to your
   taste
Oregano, to taste
(experiment with spices and
   herbs you like)

Place Tamari, olive oil and vinegar in a blender or a food processor fitted with a chopping blade and blend until thoroughly mixed (ignore the color). Add the remaining ingredients and blend until sesame seeds are completely ground. Use as a salad dressing, in soups, sandwiches, fresh fruit...everything! Makes 1¾ cups.

*Tamari is a type of soy sauce that has a pungent taste and has been aged much longer than most soy sauce.

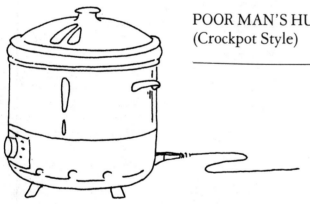

POOR MAN'S HUNGARIAN GOULASH
(Crockpot Style)

2 lbs. stew meat, cut in bite size
   cubes
1 can cream of mushroom soup
1 can cream of celery soup
1 envelope dry onion soup mix
2 cups Barbera *
1 lb. mushrooms, whole
½ cup sour cream

Place stew meat in a crockpot. Blend cream of mushroom soup, cream of celery soup, dry onion soup mix and Barbera until smooth. Pour over stew meat, cover and set crockpot on lowest setting. Cook 8 to 10 hours. Add whole mushrooms the last 15 minutes of cooking. Serve over noodles, sprinkled with dill. Top each serving with a daub of sour cream. Serves 6 generously.

*Zinfandel may be substituted for the Barbera.

"RED HOT" STEAK

4 shell (culotte) steaks, about
   ¾" thick
¼ cup olive oil
Salt and pepper, freshly ground
   to taste
½ cup Dry Marsala
½ cup Barbera*
2 large cloves garlic, finely
   chopped
½ tsp. fennel seeds
½ tsp. whole dried red chili
   pepper, finely chopped
1 Tbsps. tomato paste

Pour oil in large heavy skillet and make sure bottom is well coated. Heat oil until very hot but not smoking. Cook the steaks two to three minutes on each side. Remove to warm plates and add salt and pepper to taste. Remove all but one tablespoon of oil from skillet. Add Dry Marsala and Barbera and boil, stirring constantly, for about 30 to 40 seconds. Add garlic and fennel seeds and stir for a few more seconds. Add tomato paste and the red chili pepper and cook on low heat until sauce is fairly thick. Add steaks to sauce and cook 30 seconds on each side. Serve immediately and pour remaining sauce over steaks. Serves 4.

*Pinot Noir may be substituted for the Barbera.

DINNER IN A POT

4 to 5 lb. seven bone roast (or
   chuck)
2 large cloves garlic, cut in
   slivers
1 envelope dry onion soup mix
4 medium potatoes, peeled
6 medium carrots, cut in fourths
2 large red onions, cut in fourths
¾ lb. fresh mushrooms
2 cups Zinfandel*

Insert small pieces of garlic on both sides of roast. Rub ½ envelope onion soup mix on one side of roast. Place in large roasting pan. Rub remaining soup mix on other side of roast. Arrange potatoes, carrots, onions, around roast. Add Zinfandel. Seal tightly with foil. Place in 175° oven for six hours. Note: Due to the low cooking temperature it is important to check your oven for temperature accuracy with a good quality oven thermometer. Add whole mushrooms, recover and increase heat to 300° for additional 20 minutes. Serves 6-8.

*Ruby Cabernet may be substituted for Zinfandel.

Notes from Patti:

Slow simmering meat is not a new idea. The method was commonly used in the middle eastern culture, particularly when traveling by caravan. The cooks poured boiling oil into earthen jugs, meat was added, the jugs sealed and wrapped in goat skins. By the time the weary travelers made camp for the night the meat was ready to eat. Slow cooking is especially good for cheaper cuts of meat.

STUFFED CABBAGE ROLLS

This is an often asked for dish from both my family and friends. It takes a little work but after you have heard all the "oh's" and "ah's" at the dinner table you will make it often -- and what a wonderful way to stretch a pound of ground beef! The lemon sauce is among my most versatile recipes. It is wonderful with almost all vegetables and particularly good with lamb.

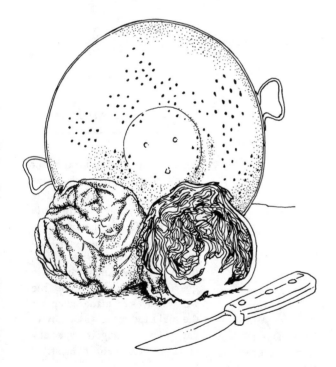

Leaves:

1 large cabbage
Enough water to cover

Stuffing:

1 lb. ground beef
1 egg
1 onion, finely chopped
¼ tsp. cinnamon
2 Tbsps. tomato sauce
½ cup Chardonnay
1 large clove garlic, finely
*   minced*
½ tsp. oregano
½ tsp. dried mint, crumbled
¾ cup uncooked rice
3 Tbsps. olive oil
Salt and freshly ground pepper,
*   to taste*

Cooking Broth:

½ cup olive oil
2 cups beef broth
1 8 oz. can tomato sauce
1 crushed bay leaf
Salt and pepper, to taste

Lemon Sauce:

3 eggs, separated
Juice of two large lemons
1 cup broth from pot
1½ tsps. arrowroot

Cut around stem in cabbage. Leave whole. Parboil in the water five minutes. Let steep for another five minutes. Remove from water and thoroughly drain. Separate whole leaves; chop smaller inside leaves and the core. Line a Dutch Oven with chopped leaves.

Combine all stuffing ingredients and mix thoroughly. Place one tablespoon of stuffing mix on each whole leaf. Fold ends of leaf over and roll up. Arrange stuffed cabbage leaves in rows in Dutch Oven. Sprinkle each layer with the ½ cup olive oil, tomato sauce and crushed bay leaf. Sprinkle lightly with salt and pepper. Add remaining tomato sauce. Add beef broth and enough water to cover. Place heavy plate on top of rolls. Cover and simmer on low heat one hour.

Beat egg whites until stiff; add egg yolks and continue beating. Add lemon juice very slowly, beating constantly. Dissolve arrowroot in a little water and mix into the cup of hot broth -- stir until thickened, heating a little if needed. Slowly add hot broth mixture to eggs, beating constantly until smooth and creamy. Remove the stuffed cabbage leaves from the pot and pour lemon sauce over them. Serves 6.

STUFFED PEPPERS BARBERA

*3 large green peppers, cut in half
  lengthwise, with seeds and
  stems removed
1 lb. lean ground round steak
½ onion, coarsely chopped
¾ cup cooked rice
½ tsp. salt
¼ tsp. pepper, freshly ground
1 tsp. Mei Yen seasoning (Spice
  Island)
2 8 oz. cans tomato sauce
1 cup Barbera (must be Barbera)
1 cup sharp cheddar cheese,
  grated*

Drop peppers in large pot of salted boiling water. Turn off heat and let stand five minutes. Drain and arrange in large casserole. Combine raw ground round steak, onion, cooked rice, salt, pepper, Mei Yen seasoning and one can tomato sauce. Stuff peppers with meat mixture. Combine remaining can tomato sauce with the Barbera. Pour over peppers. Cover and bake 40 minutes in 350° oven. Uncover, sprinkle with cheese. Return to oven, uncovered, turn off heat, and let sit about 10 minutes or until cheese has melted. Serves 6.

PARTY MEATLOAF IN CRUST

When I was very young I made this recipe because it was inexpensive, delicious and a beautiful show piece. I make it today for the same reasons, but, like everything else, it isn't as inexpensive as it use to be. However, if you compare the price of a rolled roast this is still a bargain. I make a garland of parsley interspersed with yellow daisys and arrange it around the loaf before I present it at the table.

Meatloaf:

⅔ cup evaporated milk
¾ cup Cabernet Sauvignon
6 fresh green onions, including
*   green tops, finely chopped*
¾ tsp. basil, crumbled
½ tsp. dill weed
2 tsps. salt
¼ tsp. pepper, freshly ground
3 eggs, well beaten
½ cup tomato sauce
1½ cups bread crumbs, without
*   crust*
2 lbs. ground round, ground
*   twice*

Pastry:

2 cups flour
Pinch of salt
¾ cup (1½ cubes) soft butter
*   (must be butter)*
10 Tbsps. ice water

To Assemble:

1 cup Patti's Paté (see page 17)
1 egg white, beaten

Put bread crumbs in a large mixing bowl. Add milk and mix. Add all meatloaf ingredients (except ground round). Mix carefully. Add ground round, and thoroughly mix. Cover and refrigerate for 4 to 5 hours. Shape into loaf. Place on lightly greased shallow baking pan. Bake 355° oven ½ hour. Remove and cool.

Sift flour and salt, twice into large bowl. Cut in 2 tablespoons of the butter with pastry blender until the size of peas. Add water, a little at a time and mix to a firm but pliable dough. Knead until smooth. Chill 20 minutes.

Place the rest of butter between 2 pieces of wax paper and roll to a flat pliable cake ⅛'' thick with rolling pin. The butter should be the same consistency as dough. Roll out dough to a rectangle of about 5 x 15 inches. Place the butter in the middle, fold dough over butter like a package and seal edges. Turn over.

Roll out dough to about 5 x 15 inch rectangle, fold in thirds and make a half turn to bring the dough toward you (see illustration). Repeat this step 3 times. Chill the dough one hour.

Roll to 15'' x 15'' square. Cut two 1'' strips of dough from one side. Return strips of dough to refrigerator. Place partially cooked meatloaf in center of dough. Spread thick layer of paté on top of meatloaf. Fold ends of dough over ends of loaf to about 1''. Fold one side of dough over loaf. then the other side. and pinch together. Brush thoroughly with lightly beaten egg white. Place one reserved strip of dough, cut proper length, over seam. Brush with egg white. Use the second strip to make daisies. Decorate and brush with egg white. Finish in 350° oven (pre-heated) 20-30 minutes or until golden brown. Serves 8.

GRANDMA'S CLEANING OUT FRIDGE DINNER

This hearty dish never tastes the same twice and the more vegetables the better. If using cooked left-over vegetables, add just before serving so they won't be over cooked.

> *1½ lbs. lean hamburger*
> *1 very large onion, coarsely diced*
> *2 large cloves garlic, finely*
>   *minced*
> *3 large unpeeled potatoes, cut*
>   *lengthwise and chopped in*
>   *large pieces*
> *2 8 oz. cans tomato sauce*
> *1 cup Zinfandel**
> *Salt and pepper to taste*

In large skillet sauté hamburger, with onions and garlic, until meat is barely pink. Add potatoes and stir thoroughly. Add tomato sauce and Zinfandel and again stir thouroughly. Cover, reduce heat and simmer ½ hour or until potatoes are just tender. This is the basic recipe. After adding potatoes throw in any type of vegetables you have on hand. I especially like coarsely chopped bell pepper, mushrooms and carrots. Canned whole kernel corn, drained, diced celery. I also like chili powder as a seasoning. Serves 6.

*Ruby Cabernet may be substituted for Zinfandel.

SPICE STEAK STRIPS

This is one of my personal all time favorite recipes. Although it isn't really sweet and sour it has a bit of the Orient about it. I like to prepare the recipe up to the ½ hour cooking time early in the day. Simmer 15 minutes of the ½ hour cooking time, turn off the heat and finish the rest of the cooking just before serving.

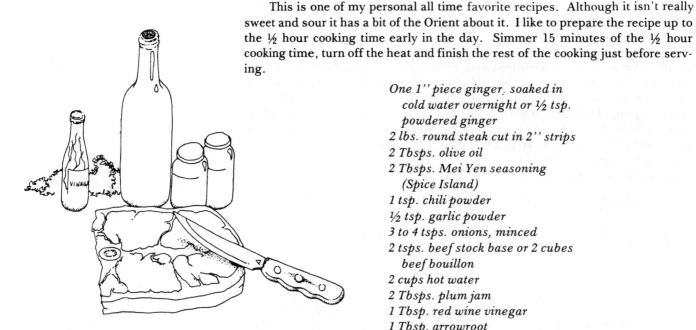

One 1" piece ginger, soaked in
* cold water overnight or ½ tsp.*
* powdered ginger*
2 lbs. round steak cut in 2" strips
2 Tbsps. olive oil
2 Tbsps. Mei Yen seasoning
* (Spice Island)*
1 tsp. chili powder
½ tsp. garlic powder
3 to 4 tsps. onions, minced
2 tsps. beef stock base or 2 cubes
* beef bouillon*
2 cups hot water
2 Tbsps. plum jam
1 Tbsp. red wine vinegar
1 Tbsp. arrowroot
1 Tbsp. cold water
3 Tbsp. Dry Sherry

Finely chop fresh ginger. Brown meat strips in oil. Add ginger (fresh or powdered), Mei Yen seasoning, chili powder, garlic powder and onions. Cook until onions are limp. Dissolve beef stock or bouillon cubes in hot water and add to beef. Add plum jam and vinegar. Cover, reduce heat to low and simmer ½ hour. Mix arrowroot in cold water -- stir until smooth. Add to meat and stir until sauce is thick. Add Dry Sherry and serve immediately. Serves 6.

ROAST VEAL WITH MARSALA AND TARRAGON BUTTER

Roast:

5 to 6 lb. rack of veal
1 Tbsp. seasoned salt (any good
* brand)*
6 Tbsps. (¾ cube) butter
¾ cup Pinot Blanc
1 cup beef stock
1 cup Dry Marsala
Salt and pepper, to taste

Tarragon Butter:

½ lb. (2 cubes) butter, softened
¼ cup fresh tarragon, minced
(must be fresh!)

Earlier in the day, mix the ½ lb. butter with tarragon and chill.
Roll veal in seasoned salt (use more if not well coated). Place on rack in baking pan. Melt the 6 tablespoons of butter, then add the Pinot Blanc and baste the roast thoroughly. Bake in 350° oven ½ hour per pound, basting often.

Remove roast from pan to heated platter. Skim off as much fat as possible from pan juices and pour remaining juices into saucepan. Add beef stock, Marsala and salt and pepper to taste. Cook over high heat until reduced to about ⅔ of original amount. Spread some of the tarragon butter on the veal and serve the roast with the sauce and extra butter. Serves 6-8.

MUSTARD ROAST

As editor and recipe-tester of this book, I was just a bit apprehensive about this roast. I love mustard, so it wasn't the 2-3 jars called for that worried me. Instead, I just couldn't imagine cooking beef for 5 to 6 hours at such a low temperature. Wouldn't it be raw? I fussed the whole time it was in the oven. The aroma was delicious, but it didn't "look" or feel like it was cooking. Finally, the 5 hours were over. I scraped the still soft mustard and salt mixture off the roast and anxiously sliced into it. It was done perfectly! The meat was pink, very succulent and permeated with a wine-mustard-salt flavor. So, be brave! I'm sure you'll enjoy this unique and delicious recipe.

Pamela Kittler

5 to 6 lb. rolled roast (this recipe
does not work well with a
smaller roast)
¾ cup Barbera (for special fla-
vor, the wine must be Barbera)
2 to 3 large jars Dijon or German
mustard
Rock salt (ice cream salt)

Soak a large piece of cheesecloth in the Barbera. Wrap roast. Place in plastic bag, seal and refrigerate for 24 hours.

Remove cheesecloth and pat roast very dry. Cover entire roast with mustard (should be at least ½" thick). Then roll the roast in rock salt to cover mustard. Place in shallow baking pan and roast at 170°, 1 hour per pound. Note: Due to the low cooking temperature, it is important to check your oven for temperature accuracy with a good quality oven thermometer.

Peel away mustard and salt crust just before serving. Serves 6 to 8.

Notes from Patti:

Very cold mustard is easier to work with. I sometimes blend Dijon and German mustard together for a little different taste. If you want to use a plain mustard, add 2 teaspoons hot Tobasco sauce per cup of mustard.

ADELINE BARGETTO OCHIPINI'S
STUFFED FLANK STEAK

Flank steak is one of the most flavorful cuts of meat when well prepared. There is, however, disagreement about the best way to cook it. Some think it should be broiled quickly, five to six minutes on each side, seasoned with salt and pepper and sliced diagonally across the grain very thinly. Others feel a flank steak should always be marinated in a good red wine. I prefer this method because not only does the wine tenderize, it adds to the flavor.

Adeline's recipe is the best I've ever tried and I sometimes change it a bit by barbecuing the flank. When I barbecue, I cook the marinade until reduced to half and pour it over the meat just before serving.

⅔ cup Zinfandel*
⅓ cup olive oil
½ tsp. oregano
½ tsp. rosemary
Salt and pepper, to taste
8 large mushrooms, thickly sliced
½ cup onions, coarsely chopped
¼ cup celery, finely chopped
2 Tbsps. butter
1 large flank steak (have butcher
  cut deep pocket)

Mix marinade of the Zinfandel, oil and herbs together. Place the flank steak in a large glass pan and pour the marinade over the meat, cover and refrigerate 6 to 8 hours, turning the meat once or twice.

Sauté mushrooms, onions and celery in the butter until tender. Drain meat, reserving marinade. Stuff vegetables into the pocket and secure edges with toothpicks. Broil 6 to 8 minutes on each side, basting with the wine marinade. Cut into thin slices diagonally across the grain. Pour pan juices over meat and serve. Serves 6.

*Ruby Cabernet may be substituted for the Zinfandel.

Fish

Your best bet for enjoying the multiple delights of the lakes and seas is to know how to select fish, and perhaps more importantly, to be familiar with your fish market. The better you know the people you are dealing with, the more assured you will be of the freshest fish in the store: the fresher the fish, the better the taste. Look the fish over carefully. Never just point to a fish and have it wrapped up. Smell it -- there should be only a slight sea smell. Touch it to feel if the fish is firm and elastic. The gills should be red and shiny and the eyes bright (if the eyes are grayish, the fish is not fresh). The scales should be bright and shiny as well. Be careful about buying frozen fish, especially the kinds that are prepackaged and sold in supermarkets. If there is a block of ice around the fish, you can be sure the fish has been partially defrosted and refrozen. If you live in a coastal area, try the wharf where fresh fish are brought in daily. Above all else *DO NOT OVERCOOK!* You do not cook fish to make it tender, you cook it to bring out the rich flavor. When any fish flakes easily with a fork, it should be served immediately to your eagerly awaiting family or friends. They will be amazed at the delicious results of your careful shopping and cooking!

CRAB SALAD FOR FOUR

2 6½ oz. cans crabmeat
8 hard boiled eggs, cut in fourths
4 firm fresh tomatoes, cut in
    eighths
2 avocados, sliced
4 Tbsps. lemon juice
8 green onions, including green
    tops, coarsely chopped
½ head iceberg lettuce, torn into
    tiny pieces
½ lb. fresh mushrooms, thinly
    sliced
18 black pitted olives
1 large bunch curley endive
    lettuce
4 large chilled dinner plates

Drain crabmeat and blot dry with paper towels. Combine iceberg lettuce, green onions and mushrooms. Brush avocado slices with lemon juice. Arrange endive leaves on plates, large ends toward edge of plates. Add iceberg lettuce combination evenly over endive leaves. Distribute ½ can of crab per plate. Arrange egg, tomato and avocado slices around plates. Garnish with black olives. Cover with plastic wrap and refrigerate at least one hour before serving. Serve with Louisiana Seafood Sauce. Serves 4 generously.

LOUISIANA SEAFOOD SAUCE

Notes from Patti:

If you like a spicy sauce add 1 tablespoon finely minced green onion, 1 teaspoon finely minced parsley and 2 tablespoons Dijon style mustard to the basic ingredients!

½ cup catsup
2 Tbsps. Dry Vermouth
1 Tbsp. lemon juice
2 Tbsps. Worcestershire sauce
⅔ cup heavy cream
Salt and freshly ground pepper,
to taste

Place all ingredients in a blender or food processor fitted with a mixing blade and blend until smooth. Refrigerate 6 to 8 hours before serving. Makes about 1½ cups.

RISOTTO WITH SHRIMP

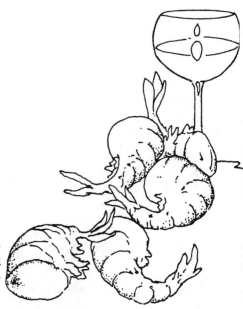

1 large onion, coarsely chopped
1 clove garlic, finely minced
6 sprigs parsley, finely minced
½ cup Dry Sherry
1 lb. fresh shrimp, unshelled
6 cups water
1½ tsps. salt
¼ lb. butter (1 cube)
¾ cup olive oil
2 cups long grain rice
Salt and white pepper, to taste

Bring the water to a rolling boil and add the 1½ teaspoons salt, onions, garlic, parsley, shrimp, Sherry and cook 5-6 minutes. Remove shrimp, peel and remove any black veins. Return shells to cooking water and simmer for 10 minutes. Line a colander with cheesecloth and strain the broth, reserving it.

Place the butter and olive oil in a large skillet; heat until a slight haze forms. Add shrimps and sauté quickly (3-4 minutes). Add rice and 1 cup of broth. Cook over medium heat, stirring continuously, adding more broth slowly as it is absorbed. Cook until rice is done - 20-25 minutes. Season with salt and white pepper to taste. Serves 4.

CREAMED SHRIMP

2 Tbsps. butter, softened
3 Tbsps. flour
1 can cream of celery soup
¾ cup Johannisberg Riesling*
2 Tbsps. lemon juice
¼ tsp. onion powder
¼ tsp. tarragon
Salt and pepper to taste
1 lb. raw shrimp, peeled and
  deveined

In a large skillet blend butter and flour until smooth over medium heat. Slowly blend in soup, Johannisberg Riesling, lemon juice and seasonings. Cook over low heat until thickened, stirring constantly. Add shrimp and cook 8 to 10 minutes.

Serve with seasoned rice. Serves 4.

*Fumé Blanc (Sauvignon Blanc) may be substituted for the Riesling.

Notes from Patti:

Rice is one food I never tire of eating. I'm sure I could enjoy it every day in one form or another. You can add almost anything to rice and it will turn out well. One of my favorite ways to cook it is to brown 1 cup long grain rice in 2 tablespoons of oil. Add 3 cups of chicken or beef stock. Cover and cook until the rice absorbs all liquid. At the point of adding liquid let your imagination take over. Try fresh parsley and pimento or fresh green onions with part of the green tops, red and green peppers and a little chopped celery. Make Spanish rice by adding tomatoes, tomato sauce, onions (lots), sliced black olives and chili powder.

SEA FOOD MAMA'S STUFFED CALAMARI

The problem with most restaurants is consistency of quality. They usually start off with a bang: well-prepared food, gracious service and terrific atmosphere. Then, little by little, portions shrink, service becomes negligent and the atmosphere dull. Not so with Sea Food Mama's of Capitola, owned by Ted and Pat Durkee who specialize in, of all things, seafood cooked over mesquite wood. I have never been disappointed with this restaurant, and order their stuffed calamari every time I find it on the menu. This recipe takes a bit of time to prepare, though it is not difficult, and is well worth the effort.

Squid:

12 small to medium size squid hoods, cleaned (see illustration). The tentacles may be finely chopped and added to the stuffing if you wish. Fresh or frozen squid may be used... about ¾ lb.

Stuffing:

½ lb. crab meat
½ lb. shrimp meat
½ cup mayonnaise
1 small green onion, finely chopped
½ tsp. Worcestershire sauce
1 Tbsp. Chenin Blanc
3 Tbsps. Parmesan cheese, grated
White pepper, to taste
6 bamboo skewers - 12 inches long each

Combine ingredients for stuffing. Then force it into the hoods (a funnel is helpful here). Thread stuffed hoods onto each skewer by going across open end of each hood to close it and then catching the tip of the closed end of the hood. Push gently to the end of the skewer and repeat; two hoods per skewer.

Place skewered, stuffed hoods on grill over hot coals and broil until *very lightly* browned -- just long enough to thoroughly heat. Over-cooking toughens Calamari. A light sprinkle of paprika may be used for color. Serve with a lemon wedge and melted butter for dipping. Serves 6.

Notes from Patti:

These can also be cooked under the broiler. Lay the skewers on a rack placed inside another pan (to catch the drippings). Cook 6-8 inches under the broiler for 1-2 minutes per side -- the flesh will stiffen and whiten slightly -- 3-4 minutes total. Soaking the skewers overnight, in water will prevent them from blackening!

SHRIMP IN SHELLS

Patti:

*I fixed your Shrimp in Shell recipe on Sunday, and found it so easy to prepare!
I used it as a cocktail hors d' oeuvre but would also be ideal as a main course.
Besides tasting delicious, it was fun to eat, although a little messy but there were
plenty of napkins. This recipe goes into my ''Special'' cookbook.*

Beverly J. Oaks, President
Santa Clara Valley Wine Growers Association

(Wine Inventory Coordinator at Almaden Vineyards, San Jose)

This dish takes no longer than 7 to 8 minutes to prepare and makes a lovely late night supper, served in bowls with sourdough bread for dipping into the sauce.

If you are having a formal dinner party, fish, in some form, is a great first course. I often make this dish at the dining table using a heavy chafing dish. The aroma alone prepares the guests for what is to come.

This is definitely a food to be eaten with the fingers. Small individual bread baskets at each plate are convenient for the shrimp shells.

> 2 lbs. large shrimps. Do not
>   remove from shells
> ¼ lb. (1 cube) butter
> 2 Tbsps. olive oil
> 4 large cloves garlic, cut length-
>   wise
> 1 cup Dry Sherry
> ½ cup parsley, coarsely chopped

Wash and thoroughly dry shrimp. In a large skillet, melt butter with olive oil over medium heat. Add garlic and brown on both sides. Discard garlic and add Sherry. Cook until there is no alcohol smell, about 2 minutes. Add shrimps and toss until shrimps are bright pink. Add parsley and toss until parsley is barely wilted. Serve immediately with sauce. Serves 6 as fish course or 4 as a main dish.

GUMBO

6 slices lean bacon, cut in fourths
2 Tbsps. olive oil
3 Tbsps. flour
3 large onions, coarsely chopped
2 cups fresh okra, thinly sliced
4 cloves garlic, finely minced
4 large tomatoes, peeled and
    chopped
1½ quarts chicken stock
1 quart clam juice
2 cups Pinot Blanc*
1 bay leaf
2 lbs. raw shrimp, shelled and
    deveined
4 hard shell crabs, quartered
1 lb. fresh crab meat
2 dashes Tabasco sauce
2-3 dashes Worcestershire
    sauce
3-4 Tbsps. parsley, finely minced
Salt and pepper, to taste

Sauté bacon in large skillet until transparent (do not brown). Remove to paper towels, reserve fat. In small pan heat 2 tablespoons of the bacon fat with the olive oil. Stir in flour to make paste. To remaining bacon fat in large skillet add onions, okra, and garlic, and sauté until onions are golden. Add tomatoes and cook uncovered until liquid has been absorbed. Add the oil/flour paste and blend until smooth. Pour all of the above into a large pot. Add chicken stock, clam juice, Pinot Blanc and bay leaf. Simmer for ½ hour. Add shrimp and hard shell crab. Simmer ½ hour. Add bacon, crab meat, Tabasco, Worcestershire and salt and pepper to taste. Simmer until thoroughly heated. Sprinkle with parsley and serve over hot rice. Serves 6 generously.

French Colombard may be substituted for the Pinot Blanc.

CHOWDER BLANC

Soup:

1 lb. fresh, firm white fish
2 cups scrubbed potatoes, cubed
    (leave peel on)
2 cups water
1 cup Pinot Blanc*
1 small onion, finely diced
¾ cup celery, FINELY chopped
2 cups evaporated milk or light

cream (I prefer cream)
1 tsp. smoked salt
3 Tbsps. butter
Salt and pepper, to taste

Garnish:

½ tsp. rosemary

Remove skin and bone from fish, and cut in small cubes. Place all ingredients except last four in large pot. Simmer until fish and potatoes are done -- about ½ hour. Add remaining ingredients and heat to bubbling. Garnish each serving with tiny pinch of crushed rosemary. Serves 4.

*Johannisberg Riesling may be substituted for the Pinot Blanc.

CIOPPINO (CHO-PEEN-O)

1 large onion, sliced
8 fresh green onions including
green tops, thinly sliced
1 green pepper, seeded and
diced
3 whole cloves garlic, peeled
⅓ cup olive oil
⅓ cup parsley, finely chopped
1 1 lb. can tomato purée
1 8 oz. can tomato sauce
*1½ cups Zinfandel**
1½ cups water
1 bay leaf
1 Tbsp. salt
¼ tsp. white pepper
⅛ tsp. dried rosemary
⅛ tsp. thyme
2 crabs 1½ to 2 lbs. each,
cleaned and cracked
18 clams, well scrubbed
1½ lbs. large shrimp in shells,
well washed

Pour olive oil in a large skillet, add all onions, green pepper and garlic and sauté over medium heat just until onions are transparent. Add parsley, tomato purée and tomato sauce, Zinfandel, water, bay leaf, salt, pepper, rosemary and thyme. Cover and simmer gently for one hour. Place the clean cracked crabs in an 8 quart pan. Cover the crabs with the clams and top with the shrimp.

Remove the garlic and bay leaf from the sauce and discard. Pour the sauce over the shell fish, cover and simmer gently for 15-20 minutes or until the clams open. Serve immediately. Serves 6 generously.

*Pinot Noir may be substituted for the Zinfandel.

RED SNAPPER MOUSSE

Fish:

1 lb. fresh Red Snapper
¼ tsp. salt
¼ tsp. white pepper
2 Tbsps. lemon juice
2 Tbsps. butter

Mousse Base:

1½ cups milk, at room tempera-
    ture
1 thick slice red sweet onion
1 bay leaf, fresh if possible
½ tsp. white pepper
3 Tbsps. butter
1 tsp. paprika
2 Tbsps. flour
1 envelope unflavored gelatin
⅓ cup Pinot Blanc*
½ cup heavy cream
1 egg white
Salt and pepper to taste

Remove skin of fish and clean the snapper with cold, running water. Pat dry. Butter shallow baking dish with a tablespoon of the butter. Add snapper and sprinkle with salt, pepper and lemon juice; dot with remaining tablespoon of butter. Cover tightly and bake 15 minutes in 350° oven. Allow fish to cool. Drain on paper towels. Shred fish and blend in a blender or a food processor fitted with a chopping blade until smooth. Set aside.

Heat milk with onion, bay leaf and pepper. Turn off heat and let stand ½ hour. Strain and discard onion and bay leaf.

Melt the 3 tablespoons butter in large skillet. Add paprika and blend thoroughly, stirring 30-40 seconds. Remove from heat and blend in flour until smooth. Add the seasoned milk and cook on low heat until sauce boils (stir constantly). Pour sauce into a large bowl and let cool.

Sprinkle gelatin over the Pinot Blanc in a large bowl (set in another bowl of hot water to help dissolve). Add sauce to pureéd fish a little at a time. Add fish mixture to dissolved gelatin and blend. Add salt and white pepper to taste. In separate bowls beat cream and egg white until stiff. Fold cream and egg white into fish mixture. Pour into lightly oiled 6-8 cup mold. Refrigerate until firm, about 3 hours. Turn on platter lined with curly endive -- garnish with twist of lemon, sliced paper thin. Serves 6.

*French Colombard may be substituted for the Pinot Blanc.

GARLIC AND ANCHOVY SAUCE (BAGNA CAUDA)

I love this dish but don't often serve it. No amount of toothpaste and breath sprays will eradicate the aroma of garlic. But do try this when you don't have to be around people for about 24 hours!

½ lb. (2 cubes) butter
5 Tbsps. olive oil
10 large cloves garlic, finely
  minced
8 anchovy fillets, coarsely
  chopped

In a large skillet heat the butter and olive oil together. Add the garlic and sauté about 1 minute over low heat. Remove the pan from heat. Add anchovies and stir well. Return the pan to the heat and cook until the anchovies are completely dissolved. Pour into a chafing dish and serve with fresh raw vegetables, celery, peppers, mushrooms, cherry tomatoes, and fresh sourdough bread. Serves 4.

SPICED FRIED FISH

2½ to 3 lbs. of any firm fleshed
  fish, such as Sea Bass, Pom –
  pano, Haddock or Red Snap-
  per, sliced in about ¾'' strips
2 large cloves garlic, finely
  minced
½ large green chili, seeded and
  finely minced
½'' piece fresh ginger root,
  grated
½ tsp. salt
1 cup flour
½ cup corn oil

Combine fish with garlic, chili, ginger root and salt. Set aside, at room temperature for ½ hour. Roll fish in flour until well coated. Heat oil in large skillet until a slight haze forms. Fry fish quickly, on both sides, and serve immediately. Serves 6.

FRIDAY NIGHT SPECIAL

12 prawns, shelled and deveined
12 scallops
3 cups cooked crab meat
1 Tbsp. butter
4 green onions including green
  tops, coarsely chopped
3 Tbsps. parsley, finely chopped
3 sprigs fresh tarragon, finely
  chopped
Salt and pepper, to taste
3 Tbsps. olive oil
¼ cup Dry Vermouth

Coat the bottom and sides of a large casserole dish with the butter and fill with sea food. Top with green onions, parsley, tarragon, salt and pepper to taste. Dribble with olive oil and Dry Vermouth. Bake in a preheated 400° oven for 10-15 minutes. For a formal dinner party, divide into 4 individual casserole dishes, and bake for only 10 minutes. Serves 4.

FISH FETTUCCINE

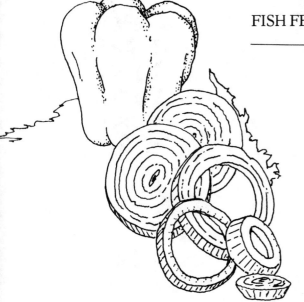

1 medium onion, very thinly
  sliced and separated into rings
1 medium green bell pepper,
  cored, seeded and finely
  minced
2 Tbsps. olive oil
1 1 lb. can Italian plum toma-
  toes, coarsely chopped
  (reserve juice)
½ cup Barbera*
1 lb. haddock fillets, cut into bite
  size cubes
Salt and pepper, to taste
1 lb. fettuccine noodles
1 Tbsp. parsley, finely minced

Pour olive oil in a large skillet. Add onion rings and bell pepper. Cook over medium heat until onions are transparent. Add tomatoes, reserved tomato juice, Barbera and salt and pepper to taste, lower heat and simmer, uncovered, 15 minutes. Add fish and simmer additional 10 minutes.

Cook fettuccine until al dente. Transfer to a deep serving dish. Add sauce and mix well. Top with parsley and serve at once. Serves 4.

*Pinot Noir may be substituted for the Barbera.

AVOCADO SURPRISE

1 6½ oz. can of tuna, packed in
   water, well drained
4 Tbsps. green onions, finely
   chopped
2 hard boiled eggs, coarsely
   chopped
3 Tbsps. Dry Vermouth
2 large firm avocados, chilled,
   halved and pitted
4 tsps. lemon juice
16 cherry tomatoes
1 large lemon, cut in fourths,
   and seeded

Combine tuna, onions, eggs and Dry Vermouth and chill at least an hour. Rub 1 teaspoon lemon juice over cut edges and cavities of each avocado half. Spoon tuna mixture into avocados and garnish each serving with 4 cherry tomatoes and 1 wedge of lemon. Serves 4.

EASY BOUILLABAISSE

1 lb. flounder fillets, cubed
1 lb. mackerel fillets, cubed
1 lb. halibut, fillets, cubed
5 fresh or canned Italian plum
   tomatoes, peeled and quartered
5 unpeeled potatoes, boiled and
   cubed
1 medium onion, thinly sliced
2 cloves garlic, finely minced
3 sprigs parsley, finely minced
1 bay leaf
2 tsps. lemon rind, grated
8 cups boiling water
Salt and pepper, to taste
½ cup French Colombard*

Place the fish, tomatoes, potatoes, onion, garlic, parsley, bay leaf and lemon rind in a large soup kettle (or use a six quart dutch oven) and pour in the boiling water. Bring to a slow boil, add the French Colombard and reduce heat. Simmer until the fish flakes easily -- 15-20 minutes. Serves 6.
   *Pinot Blanc may be substituted for the French Colombard.

BAKED FILLETS OF SOLE

2 lbs. fillets of sole
1 Tbsp. butter
½ cup Fumé Blanc*
1 Tbsp. parsley, finely chopped
½ tsp. salt
¼ tsp. white pepper
8-10 fresh mushrooms, cut in half

Butter shallow baking dish. Arrange fillets of sole in dish. Combine Fumé Blanc, parsley, salt and pepper. Pour over sole. Arrange mushroom halves around sole. Cover. Bake 15 minutes in a 450° oven. Serves 4.

*Pinot Blanc or a dry Johannisberg Riesling may be substituted for the Fumé Blanc.

SHARK STEAKS IN FOIL TENTS

Shark is without a doubt the most overlooked fish in the United States. It is delicious and inexpensive. It is used commercially for frozen scallops and products called fish fillets. Shark is greatly appreciated in Europe and the Far East. So introduce yourself with this recipe!

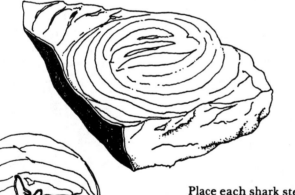

4 shark steaks
1 small shallot, sliced paper thin
12 large mushrooms, thinly sliced
2 tsps. parsley, finely minced
4 tsps. lemon juice
8 Tbsps. Gewürztraminer*
4 double thick pieces of foil, large enough to enclose each steak

Place each shark steak on a double thickness of aluminum foil. Divide shallots, mushrooms and parsley into 4 equal parts, and sprinkle over top of steaks. Bring up sides and ends of foil. Pour 1 teaspoon lemon juice and 2 tablespoons Gewürztraminer over each steak. Bring foil together, tent style, and seal. Place in a preheated 375° oven for 15-20 minutes (depending on thickness of the steaks). Remove from foil and serve immediately, garnished with lemon slices. Serves 4.

*Chenin Blanc may be substituted for Gewürztraminer.

Desserts

I have always had a somewhat different approach to desserts. For instance, I never serve rich desserts at dinner parties; after five or six courses one doesn't need, and often doesn't want, rich caloric food. So I save rich desserts for one dish meals, like a beef stew.

In an age when everyone is so health and weight conscious I have come to rely heavily on fresh fruits, cheeses and the fine dessert wines of California. These wines offer an infinite variety of taste sensations: everything from a light, crisp Chenin Blanc to a full bodied late harvest Johannisberg Riesling. In addition, there are some truly great fortified dessert wines, such as Ports and Cream Sherrys, which also lend themselves to the flavors of fruit, cheese and even nuts. So as ingredient or accompaniment, try a bit of wine for dessert.

RAZAMATAZ ONE

*California White Champagne,
well chilled
Raspberry Wine, well chilled*

My good and true (and often threatening) editor keeps impressing on me the importance of measurements. Well, this time I just can't do it. The best method is to mix until the color is a nice deep shade of raspberry. Of course a magnum of White Champagne to a 4/5 qt. bottle of Raspberry Wine is perfect.

RAZAMATAZ TWO

To ½ glass of Razamataz One add on large scoop frozen Raspberry Sherbet. Top each serving with six fresh raspberries that have been placed in the freezer for 1-2 hours.

GRAPES AMABILE

This recipe is elegant and no work. The grapes become plump with the wine while taking on the flavor as well. A diamond optic bowl glass is especially pretty to use. I use my two tined fish forks to spear the grapes. It is important to cover the grapes tightly since exposing the wine to air will cause the wine to oxidize.

*2 lbs. Thompson seedless grapes
1 4/5 qt. Moscato Amabile*

Wash, dry and stem grapes. Place in a large serving bowl and pour the whole bottle of Moscato Amabile over grapes and *cover tightly*. Refrigerate 72 hours. No cheating! Serve in large wine glasses.

PATTI'S FRUIT BOWL

It simply isn't "Holiday" time at our house until I turn out the first of several fruit bowls for family and friends.

1 large can peach halves
1 large can pear halves
1 large can pineapple chunks
1 lb. pitted prunes
Maraschino cherries
1 4/5 qt. bottle Chenin Blanc*
1 cup Brandy

Drain fruit. Place a prune in each peach half, and a cherry in each pear half. Arrange in an attractive design around the sides of a clear glass bowl or giant brandy snifter. Fill center with pineapple chunks and remaining prunes. Pour in Chenin Blanc and Brandy. Cover tightly with plastic wrap and refrigerate at least 24 hours. 48 hours is even better! Serves 8 to 10.
    *A light sweet Muscat wine may be substituted for Chenin Blanc.

POACHED PEARS AMABILE

2 cups Moscato Amabile*
2 cups water
1½ cups sugar
1 whole orange peel, cut in thin
    strips
1 cinnamon stick
3 to 4 cloves
6 large fresh pears (with stems)

Put Moscato Amabile, water, sugar, and orange peel, cinnamon stick and cloves in large saucepan and cook on low heat until sugar begins to dissolve; raise the heat and boil 8 to 10 minutes.
    While syrup cooks, peel pears, being careful to leave the stems on. Slice a small bit off each bottom so that pears can stand securely upright. Add pears and poach until tender, but firm, 10-15 minutes. Arrange on dessert plates, pour equal amounts of syrup over each serving. Decorate with sprigs of fresh mint. Serves 6.
    *A *sweet* Chenin Blanc may be substituted for Moscato Amabile.

Notes from Patti:

NEVER, NEVER discard orange or lemon peelings. Remove and discard as much of the white membrane as possible, as it tends to be bitter. Wash and dry the peelings. Place on cookie sheet and dry on the very lowest heat of your oven—150° for 3 hours, 170° for 2 to 2½ hours. Grind in a blender and store in small jars. Will keep 3 to 4 months.

BANANAS WITH PORT CUSTARD SAUCE

Sauce:

2 large eggs
¾ cup fine sugar
1 cup Tawny Port
1 thick slice of lemon
1 cinnamon stick

Bananas:

4 peeled bananas, sliced length-
wise
2 Tbsps. butter
8 coconut macaroons, crumbled

Beat eggs and sugar until fluffy. Heat Tawny Port with lemon and cinnamon stick to the boiling point. Remove lemon and cinnamon. Pour into egg and sugar mixture, a bit at a time, until well blended. Pour into the top of a double boiler and cook until thick, stirring constantly.

Sauté bananas in butter and remove to warm platter. Sprinkle with about ¾ of the coconut macaroon pieces and ladle sauce over bananas and cookies. Sprinkle remaining cookie pieces over top as garnish. Serves 4.

CREAM SHERRY PEACHES

¼ cup apricot jam
1 tsp. orange peel, grated
3 Tbsps. fine sugar
½ cup water
4 large ripe peaches, peeled,
halved, and seeded
¼ cup Cream Sherry

In medium saucepan, combine apricot jam, orange peel, sugar and water. Cook, stirring constantly, over low heat, until mixture is syrupy -- about 5-6 minutes. Add peach halves to syrup and simmer until tender -- about 10 minutes. Add Cream Sherry and gently mix in. Remove to serving bowl, cover and refrigerate 4 to 5 hours before serving. Serves 4.

BROILED GRAPEFRUIT WITH ALMOND MARSALA

This is one of those simple but elegant foods that takes only minutes to prepare. Use as a dessert, a brunch dish, as a snack.

2 grapefruit, cut in half, seeded
and sectioned
4 level tsps. light brown sugar
8 Tbsps. Almond Marsala*

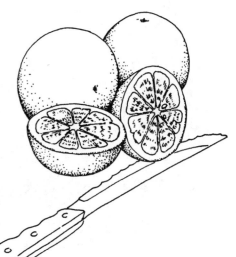

Sprinkle each half grapefruit with 1 teaspoon light brown sugar; tap sugar into grapefruit with the back of a spoon. Drizzle 2 tablespoons Almond Marsala over each half grapefruit. Broil until bubbling and brown. Serves 4.
*Amaretto may be substituted for Almond Marsala.

CUSTARD A LA ALMOND MARSALA

4 large eggs
½ cup fine sugar
2 cups milk
6 Tbsps. Almond Marsala*
6 Tsps. almonds, grated

Beat eggs and sugar together until light and double in volume (about five minutes). Stir in milk slowly until well mixed. Pour into six well buttered custard cups (any individual cups that are oven-proof and hold ¾ cup will do) and cover with foil. Place the cups in shallow pan and fill the pan about ⅓ full with boiling water. Place the pan in pre-heated 350° oven and bake five minutes. Reduce heat to 275° and bake ½ hour. Drizzle one tablespoon Almond Marsala over each cup and continue to bake an additional ½ hour. Unmold and sprinkle each custard with one teaspoon grated almonds. Serves 6.
*Amaretto may be substituted for Almond marsala.

Notes from Patti:

Eggs and milk should always be brought to room temperature before using.

To determine when custard is done, insert knife about one inch from edge of cup. Knife should come out clean.

Always cover custards during baking, otherwise a hard skin will form and the custard will shrink.

STRAWBERRY MARSALA MOUSSE

1 pint fresh strawberries,
washed, hulled and puréed
in blender or food processor
1 pint fresh strawberries, washed
and hulled
1 cup sifted confectioners sugar
2 tsps. unflavored gelatin
6 Tbsps. Strawberry Marsala*
1 pint heavy cream, stiffly
whipped

Sprinkle puréed pint of strawberries with the confectioners sugar and mix in until sugar is dissolved. Set aside. Reserve 8 of the best whole strawberries for garnish. Cut the rest of the whole strawberries in half and set aside. Pour 3 tablespoons Strawberry Marsala in small saucepan and sprinkle with gelatin; add rest of Strawberry Marsala to the gelatin mixture and heat, stirring constantly, over low heat 3 to 4 minutes or until gelatin is dissolved. Set aside and cool to room temperature. Combine with the puréed strawberries. Gently fold the purée into the whipped cream. Pour into a chilled 1½ quart mold. Insert the strawberry halves throughout mousse. Cover with foil and refigerate until firm. Turn out on serving plate and decorate with whole strawberries. Makes 6 generous servings or 8 skimpy servings.

*Any strawberry liqueur can be substituted for Strawberry Marsala.

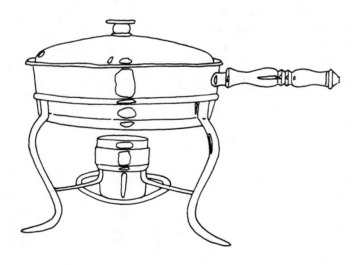

Dear Patti:

Here is a truly beautiful Chocolate Mousse. Its nose is full of chocolate with undertones of coffee and citrus. The texture is light and yet it is full-bodied. Ah, but the aftertaste! Here, the complexities of the chocolate, coffee, and orange all come together in a perfect wedding of flavors, with the excitement that a bit of alcohol always brings to cooking.

It was my pleasure to make and taste-test this recipe in my kitchen. I marvelled at its simplicity and how quickly this Mousse went together. Licking the spoon gave me a preview of what was to come later.

If only restaurants would serve Mousse like this instead of the box pudding with spray can whipped cream that most of them carry on their menus. Surely, people would rather pay more for a quality dessert. Surprisingly, this recipe takes no more time than the glue mixture that is often served. A recipe like this will take Chocolate Mousse off the endangered species list.

Sincerely,

Bernie Turgeon
Chocolate Moussekateer
Turgeon & Lohr Winery

SIMPLE AND SINFUL CHOCOLATE MOUSSE

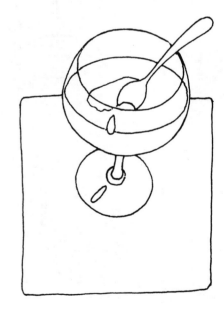

1-6 oz. package semi-sweet
  chocolate chips
2 Tbsps. Coffee Marsala*
1 Tbsp. Orange Marsala
1 tsp. vanilla
2 eggs plus 2 egg yolks
¼ cup sugar
½ pint heavy cream

Melt chocolate with the Coffee Marsala and Orange Marsala in the top of a double boiler and set aside. Put the eggs and yolks, vanilla and sugar in blender or food processor fitted with a mixing blade and blend, at medium speed, for three minutes. Add the cream and blend, until smooth, then add chocolate mixture, blending until just mixed in completely. Pour into 6 cream pots (or any other ½ cup container) and refrigerate for six hours. Serves 6. (This recipe *cannot* be sucessfully doubled. If more is desired, make two batches.)
*Kahlua may be substituted for Coffee Marsala.

GREAT AUNT MARY'S CHEESECAKE

Notes from Patti:

When Great Aunt Mary made her cheesecake, it was for special occasions because it took time and work to make. With the help of my food processor, I put it together in about 10 minutes.

If using a food processor, place the chopping blade in work bowl and cream the cheese, sugar, vanilla, lemon rind, limon juice and egg yolks until smooth. Pour into mixing bowl and continue with the remaining steps.

Jim Piles is my friend and literary agent. He both encouraged and cajoled me to write this book because he found my recipes so simple to prepare:

"If you have used any of the other recipes in this book, you know that they are simple to prepare and virtually fool-proof. I am living testimony that this cheesecake recipe is idiot-proof. My spring-form pan is larger than the one called for in the recipe, so I decided to increase the recipe by 50%. Instead of using three eggs, I forgot and used four. The cake was great. The next time I prepared the cheesecake, instead of following directions, I was in a hurry and threw all the ingredients into the food processor at once. The cake was not as fluffy as the previous one, but my guests still thought it was great. Anyone who can devise recipes that I cannot screwup is a genius!"

Jim Piles

Crust:

1½ cups Zwiebach crumbs
3 Tbsps. butter, melted
2 Tbsps. sugar

Filling:

1 lb. cream cheese, at room
   temperature
½ cup sugar
½ tsp. vanilla
Rind of one lemon, grated
1 Tbsp. lemon juice
2 large eggs, separated

Topping:

1 Tbsp. sugar
½ tsp. vanilla
1 cup sour cream

Mix the Zwiebach crumbs with melted butter and the 2 tablespoons sugar. Press into the bottom of a 9" spring-form pan. Place in a 275° oven for 5 minutes. Remove and cool.

Cream the cheese with the sugar, vanilla, lemon rind and lemon juice until smooth. Add egg yolks, one at a time, and cream until smooth. In a separate bowl, beat the egg whites until stiff. Gently fold the egg whites into the cheese mixture. Pour mixture over the crumb base and bake in a 300° oven for 45 minutes.

Blend the sugar and vanilla into the sour cream. Spread over the top of cheesecake and return to the oven for an additional 10 minutes. Cool and remove the ring of the pan to serve. This is a very rich dessert, so serve small pieces! Serves 10 to 12.

MOKA MARSALA NO-BAKE COOKIES

1 6 oz. package semi-sweet
chocolate chips
¼ cup sugar
3 Tbsps. light corn syrup
½ cup Moka Marsala
2½ cups vanilla wafers, finely
crushed
1 cup walnuts, finely chopped
1 cup powdered sugar, sifted

Melt chocolate in the top of a double boiler over simmering water, stirring until chocolate is melted. Remove from heat, add sugar, corn syrup and Moka Marsala and blend thoroughly. Combine crushed vanilla wafers and chopped walnuts in a large mixing bowl. Add chocolate mixture and mix well. Form into 1'' balls and roll in powdered sugar. Place in an airtight canister and allow to sit for several days. Makes 3 dozen.

APRICOT WINE BREAD

I like this bread best when it is a day old, I also find it freezes well. Great for brown bagging or mid-afternoon snacking.

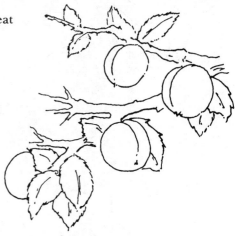

3 cups oatmeal
8 oz. yogurt
½ cup Apricot Wine
½ cup butter (1 cube), melted
½ cup sugar
2 large eggs
1½ cups flour
¾ cup dried apricots, chopped
2 tsps. baking powder
½ tsp. baking soda
½ tsp. salt
4 16 oz. tin cans, buttered

Combine cereal, yogurt and Apricot wine in a large bowl. Mix well and let stand a few minutes to allow cereal to absorb liquid. Add butter, sugar and eggs and mix until well blended. In a separate bowl, add flour, apricots, baking powder, salt and baking soda and mix thoroughly. Add to cereal mixture, mixing just until dry ingredients are moistened. Divide mixture between the 4 buttered cans and bake on middle rack at 350° oven for 45 to 50 minutes. Cool before removing from cans. Makes 4 loaves.

GAYLE'S GENOISE

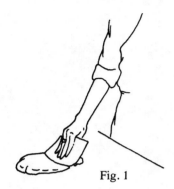

Fig. 1

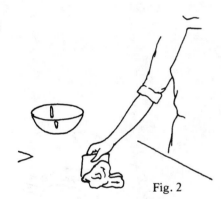

Fig. 2

Fig. 3

Gayle's French bakery is the only place in town where people wait in long lines without complaining, and that is because Joe and Gayle Ortiz are the finest pastry makers I've ever met. A number of years ago, Gayle apprenticed herself to a well known San Francisco pastry chef. Eventually she and Joe went to France; not to school -- they were beyond that, but to work in some of the finest bakeries in Paris. Now she has her own bakery in the small village of Capitola. Gayle graciously reworked this delicious creation so that it can be made in most home kitchens.

Cake:

7 eggs, at room temperature
1 cup sugar
½ cup cocoa
½ cup flour
¼ lb. (1 cube) sweet butter

Syrup:

1 cup water
½ cup sugar
½ cup Strawberry Marsala

Whipping Cream:

2 cups heavy cream
4 Tbsps. Strawberry Marsala
2 Tbsps. sugar

Strawberry Topping:

*1 basket strawberries, washed
and hulled*
3 Tbsps. red current jelly

Chocolate Sheeting:

*9 oz. semi-sweet
    chocolate, grated (be sure to
    use real chocolate, not a
    chocolate flavored imitation)*
⅓ cup corn syrup

Pre-heat oven to 350°

Melt butter, set aside. Sift cocoa and flour together, set aside. Mix eggs and 1 cup sugar in a stainless steel bowl and set over boiling water, whisking constantly to prevent the eggs from cooking. Warm the eggs until just warmer than your hand, then beat for 15 minutes until the mixture triples in volume and is cold (it should look like whipped cream). Sift the cocoa/flour mixture a little at a time into the egg mixture and fold it gently. Fold one third of the batter into the butter, then fold the butter mixture back into remaining batter. Divide the batter in half and pour into two 9'' greased and floured cake pans. Bake immediately for 20 to 30 minutes until cake springs back when pressed with your fingertip. Use one layer for this recipe (save other layer for another use -- it freezes beautifully).

While cake is baking, melt chocolate in a double boiler. Add corn syrup and mix well. Set aside for 30 minutes.

Boil 1 cup water and ½ cup sugar for two minutes. Cool and add ½ cup Strawberry Marsala. Set aside. Whip cream until soft peaks, then add two tablespoons sugar and four tablespoons Strawberry Marsala and whip until stiff.

Place the chocolate mixture onto a smooth surface (a chilled marble is perfect). Knead until the mixture stiffens, about three minutes. Shape into a rectangle 3'' x 6'' and let rest 15 minutes. (see figures 1-3).

With a large serrated knife (such as a bread knife), slice the cooled cake into three equal layers. Brush the first layer liberally with the syrup. Invert the layer onto a platter and brush the other side with syrup. Spread a thin layer of the whipped cream on the layer. Repeat syrup and whipped cream on the middle and top layers, mounding the cream over the top layer and sides (semi-spherical). Chill. (see figures 4-11).

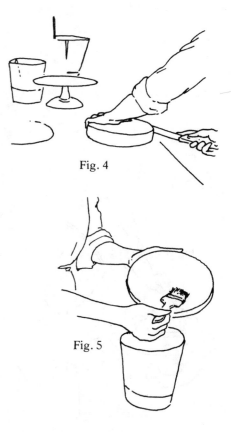

Fig. 4

Fig. 5

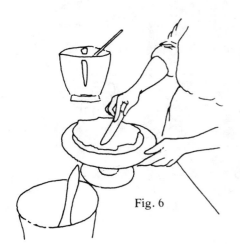

Fig. 6

Fig. 7

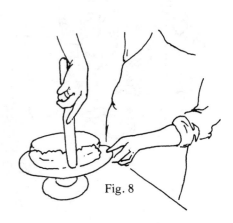

Fig. 8

Place strawberries in a single layer tightly next to each other in the center of the top of the cake. Slice the chocolate into 1'' strips. Set one strip into a hand or electric pasta machine and flatten it to medium thickness. Place the chocolate sheet around the edge of the cake. Roll another chocolate strip and continue to wrap the sheeting around the cake. Continue rolling each chocolate strip one at a time and place each successive sheet inside the next, following the contours of the cake inward, folding the top edge of each sheet a bit outward -- petal like. Chocolate should cover cake up to the strawberry center (see figures 12-17).

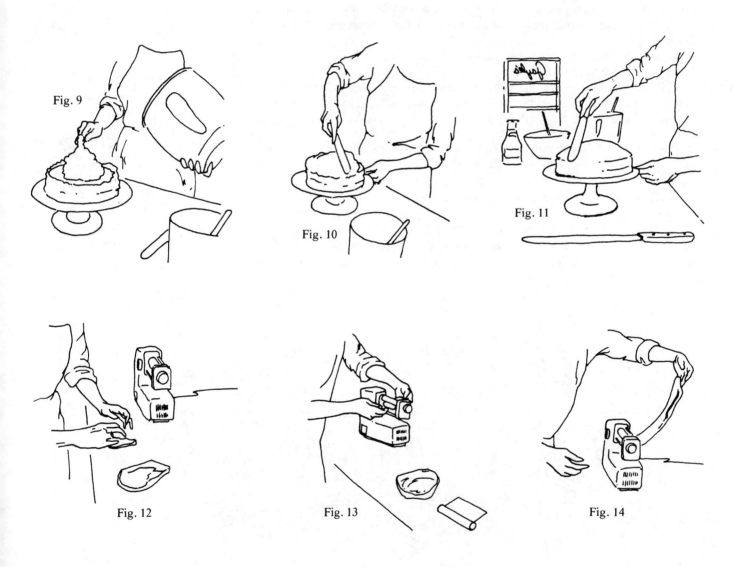

Fig. 9

Fig. 10

Fig. 11

Fig. 12

Fig. 13

Fig. 14

Boil current jelly until melted, stirring until smooth. Glaze strawberries with the jelly using a pastry brush. (see figure 18). Chill until serving (should be served the same day it is prepared). Serves 8 to 10.

Editor's note: Leave it to Patti to discover even a dessert recipe that uses a pasta machine! Although the chocolate could be rolled out by hand if you work quickly, the pasta machine is helpful and fun. Though this dessert may seem complicated, each step is easy and it is worth the time spent preparing it. This cake is spectacular.

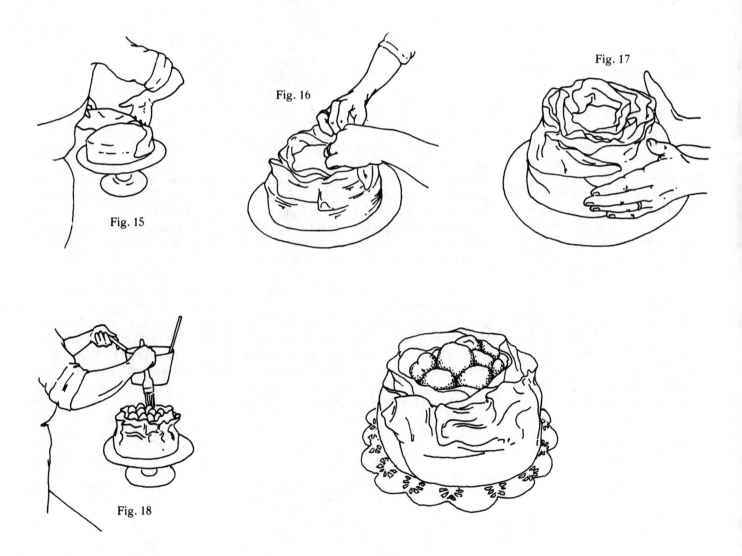

Fig. 15

Fig. 16

Fig. 17

Fig. 18

COOKING CLASS ICE-BOX CAKE

*3 8'' circles cut from cooking
   parchment paper
4 large egg whites, room temperature
⅛ tsp. salt
¼ tsp. cream of tartar
½ cups sugar
1 6 oz. package semi-sweet
   chocolate chips
4 Tbsps. Orange Marsala
2 pints fresh strawberries,
   stemmed, washed and thickly
   sliced (3 slices per berry)
   set aside 6 whole berries for
   decoration
1½ pints heavy cream
½ cup powdered sugar*

Notes from Patti:

This recipe is the result of one of my cooking classes. I am usually well prepared for my students but one evening I simply forgot about dessert. I suggested to my class that we create something different and exciting, but it had to include four egg whites I needed to use before they spoiled. Someone suggested meringue cookies to which we all booed and hissed loudly; however, the meringue was a good idea and I had chocolate and fresh strawberries on hand. What goes with chocolate and strawberries? Whipped cream, of course! The result is our Cooking Class Ice Box cake.

Beat egg whites with salt and cream of tartar until stiff. Gradually add sugar and beat meringue until stiff and glossy. Divide meringue between the three parchment circles and spread to ¼'' thick. Place on cookie sheet and bake in 250° oven for 25 minutes. (Meringue should be pale gold in color.) Remove from oven and peel off parchment paper, place on racks to dry.

Place chocolate chips and Orange Marsala in top of double boiler and melt, stirring constantly.(Never allow inset of double boiler to touch the boiling water. This will make the chocolate grainy).

Whip cream until stiff, gradually adding sugar. Continue to beat until cream is very stiff.

Place one meringue on cake plate and spread with a thick layer of melted chocolate. Allow chocolate to cool and cover with a layer of sliced strawberries. Spread a thick layer of whipped cream over berries, add second meringue and repeat the above steps. Top with third meringue and spread with remaining chocolate. Ice sides of cake with remaining whipped cream. Decorate top with whole strawberries. Refrigerate 2 to 3 hours. Serves 8.

CREAM SHERRY WALNUTS

1½ cups sugar
½ tsp. salt
¼ cup honey
½ cup water
2 tsps. Cream Sherry
3 cups walnut halves
1 large shallow pan, lined with
   a double thickness of waxed
   paper

Place the sugar, salt, honey, and water in a large saucepan and bring to a boil. Continue to cook until syrup reaches a firm-soft stage, about 250° on a candy thermometer (about 4 to 5 minutes). Stir in Cream Sherry. Remove from heat, add walnut halves and mix thoroughly. Turn into pan and spread in a single layer. Cool 2 to 3 hours and cut into pieces. Serves 6 to 8.

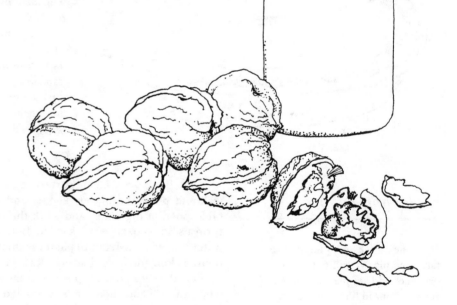

SWEET VERMOUTH PUMPKIN PIE

This is my very favorite pumpkin pie; however, I will change it around once in a while by substituting Cream Sherry or Honey Wine for the Sweet Vermouth.

Sweet Pastry:

2 cups self-rising flour
¼ lb. (1 cube) butter (at room
  temperature)
¼ cup fine sugar
1 large egg yolk
1-2 Tbsps. cold water
1 egg white, lightly beaten

Filling:

1½ cups pumpkin purée
⅔ cup dark brown sugar, firmly
  packed
1¼ tsps. ground cinnamon
½ tsp. ground ginger
¼ tsp. ground nutmeg
¼ tsp. salt
1 cup evaporated milk
1 cup Sweet Vermouth
3 eggs, well beaten

Notes from Patti:

A neat trick for liquid or custard type pies -- pull out middle over rack and set pie shell in the center. Pour in filling and gently push rack in place. Nary a spilled drop!

Sift flour on a clean surface and shape into a large ring. Form a high wall and place the butter, sugar, and egg yolk in center of the ring. Add 1 tablespoon of the water and work the central mixture with two table knives to form a smooth paste. Work in the flour from the inside of the ring, adding more water if needed. Mix until pastry is thick and light to the touch. Place on lightly floured cloth and cover loosely. Refrigerate one hour before using.

Fit Pastry into a 9'' pie pan, making a high fluted edge. Brush with egg white and chill one hour. Pre-heat oven at 450°

Place all filling ingredients in blender or food processor fitted with a chopping blade and blend until sugar is dissolved and mixture is smooth. Pour into the pastry shell and bake 10 minutes on center oven rack at 450°. Reduce heat to 350° and continue to bake for ½ hour.

Index

The Wine Appreciation Guild Books
"The Classic Series on Cooking With Wine"

This series of wine cookbooks is the largest collection of cooking with wine recipes available in the World. There is no duplication of features or recipes in the Wine Advisory Board Cookbooks. Specific wine types are recommended as table beverages for all main dishes. The present series represents over 4,000 different recipes of all types using wine. From wine cocktails, hors d'oeuvres, salads, soups, wild game, fish, eggs, many different main dishes to desserts and jellies; the magnitude of this collection of wine recipes is overwhelming. Who could possibly develop and test such a large number of recipes? These books are the result of the cooperation of over 400 people in the wine industry. In 1961 the Wine Advisory Board began collecting the favorite and best recipes of various winemakers and their families. Most of the recipes are old family favorites, tested with time and then retested and proven in Wine Advisory Board test kitchens. We are particularly pleased with the recipes and wine choices from staff members of the Department of Viticulture and Enology and the Department of Food and Science and Technology of University of California, Davis and Fresno.

So here is a series of the very best wine recipes; selected and developed by many of the most knowledgeable wine and food lovers of America.

#501 Gourmet Wine Cooking The Easy Way: Recipes for memorable eating, prepared quickly and simply with wine. Most of the recipes specify convenience foods which can be delightfully flavored with wine enabling the busy lay chef to set a gourmet table for family & friends with a minimum of time in the kitchen. More than 500 tested and proven recipes; used frequently by the first families of America's wine industry. 128 pp, 8 ½" x 11", illustrated 2001 edition $12.95 @ 2 ISBN 0-932664-01-6

#502 New Adventures in Wine Cookery by California Winemakers: 2001 Edition includes many new recipes from California's new winemakers. The life work of the winemakers is to guide nature in the development in wine of beauty, aroma, bouquet and subtle flavors. Wine is part of their daily diet, leading to more flavorful dishes, comfortable living, merriment and good fellowship. These recipes contributed by Winemakers, their families and colleagues represent this spirit of flavorful good living. A best selling cookbook with 500 exciting recipes including barbecue, wine drinks, salads and sauces. 128 pp, illustrated, 81/2" x 11", $12.95 @ ISBN 0-932664-10-5.

#503 Favorite Recipes of California Winemakers: The original winemaker's cookbook and a bestseller for fifteen years. Over 200 dedicated winemakers have shared with us their love of cooking. They are the authors of this book, which is dedicated to a simple truth known for thousands of years in countless countries: good food is even better with wine. Over 500 authentic recipes, many used for generations, are included in this "cookbook classic". 1986 edition. 128 pp, 81/2" x 11", illustrated, $9.95 @ ISBN 0-932664-03-2.

504 Dinner Menus with Wine by Emily Chase and Wine Advisory Board. Over 100 complete dinner menus with recommended complimentary wines. This book will make your dinner planning easy and the results impressive to your family and most sophisticated guests. Emily Chase worked with the winemakers of California a number of years and was also the Home Economics Editor of Sunset Magazine. She tested recipes for six years and is the author of numerous articles and books on cooking. This edition contains 400 different recipes, suggestions for wines to accompany dinners and tips on serving, storing and enjoying wine. 1981 Edition, 128 pp, illustrated, 8 ½" x 11", $9.95 @ ISBN 0-932664-30-x.

#554 Wine Cellar Record Book: A professionally planned, elegant, leatherette bound cellar book for the serious wine collector. Organized by the wine regions of the World, helpful for keeping perpetual inventories and monitoring the aging of each wine in your cellar. Enough space for over 200 cases of wine and space to record tasting notes and special events. Illustrated, 12" x 101/2", six ring binder, and additional pages available. $39.95 @ ISBN 0-932664-06-7.

#640 The Champagne Cookbook: "Add Some Sparkle to Your Cooking and Your Life" by Malcolm R. Hebert. Cooking with Champagne is a glamorous yet easy way to liven up your cuisine. The recipes range from soup, salads, hors d'oeuvres, fish, fowl, red meat, vegetables and of course desserts-all using Champagne. Many new entertaining ideas with Champagne cocktails, drinks and Champagne lore are included along with simple rules on cooking with and serving Sparkling Wines. California, New York and European Champagne makers and their families provide recipes. The author's 30 years of teaching and writing about food and wine makes this an elegant yet practical book. 128 pp, illustrated, 81/2" x 11", pp $14.95 @ ISBN 0-932664-65-2

#641 The Pocket Encyclopedia of California Wine: "The most useful little book on California wine yet" A convenient and thorough reference book that fits in vest pocket. Provides answers to most questions about California wines, the wineries, grape varieties and wine terms. Includes maps and a tasting note section. Handy to carry with you to restaurants, wine tastings and wine shops to make intelligent selections. Covers Arizona, Mexico and Hawaii.336 pp, 73/4" x 31/2" $14.95 @ ISBN 0-932664-40-7.

#673 The California Wine Drink Book by William I. Kaufman. Cocktails, hot drinks, punches and coolers all made with wine. Over 200 different drink recipes, using various wines along with mixing tips and wine entertaining suggestions. Today's accent on lighter drinks makes this a most useful handbook and you'll save money too by using wine rather than higher taxed liquors. Pocket size, leatherette cover, 128 pp, and $6.95, ISBN 0-932664-10-9.

#727 Wine Lovers Cookbook by Malcolm Herbert, The most unique in our Wine Cookbook Series with 100 winning recipes from the National Cooking with Wine Contest. All recipes have been tested and written for easy preparation and reliable results. They range from the Artichoke Appetizer with Wine to cold Apricot Soup, Lime-house Chicken to Pumpkin Beef Stew. And in-depth chapter on California wine, a wine & food chart and cooking tips are included. With this book in hand the magic is out of the bottle. 176 pp, illustrated, 8 ½" x 11". $12.95 @ ISBN 0-932664-82-2

 # 855 Pocket Encyclopedia of American Wine, East of the Rockies by Wm. Kaufman. Companion to the author's best-selling Pocket Encyclopedia of California Wine and other Western states. A convenient and thorough reference listing all Eastern American wineries with vital information on vineyards, winemaking practices, climates viticulture, appellations, tasting terms, visiting information and maps. Wine from

Texas and Colorado through the Midwest, the south, to New York and New England included. Also tasting notes and award winning wines. 144 pp, 7 ½" x 3 ½" gold imprinted leatherette cover. $9.95 @ ISBN 0-932664-41-5

#914 Wine, Food & the Good Life by Arlene Mueller & Dorothy Indelicato. "Celebrating 50 years of family winemaking." Here is a cookbook with generation proven, wine family recipes complemented by contemporary California cuisine recipes and wine entertaining tips. The California Wine Country lifestyle is captured through fascinating historical anecdotes from three generations of winemaking, old photos, and lots of sharing of cooking tips from the winemakers and their families. Recipes range from quick and easy to "gourmet' and represent a variety of ethnic background with Italian predominating. 144 pp, illustrated, 8 ½"x 11". $9.95 @ISBN 0-932664-47-4

#986 Fine Wine In Food by Patricia Ballard. Wine is also a food. When cooking with wine there is a complex interaction of flavors that enhance the end product. Culinary achievement requires use of the finest ingredients. Using a fine wine is also essential. Each variety varies from mild to intense in flavor so selection of the proper wine for each recipe is important. $9.95 ISBN 0-932-664-5

#6508 Pocket Encyclopedia of American Wine-Northwest by William I. Kaufman. The newest addition to Kaufman's award winning pocket encyclopedia series. Complete directory to all of the wineries in Oregon, Washington, Idaho, and Montana. Includes addresses, phone numbers, winemakers, owners and highlights on wines produced, varietals and

vineyards. An essential and handy guide to the exciting new premium wine producing area. Leatherette cover, convenient 7 ¾' x 33 ½', pp. $7.95

#6509 The Benefits of Moderate Drinking, "Alcohol, Health, and Society" by Gene Ford, foreword by Thomas B. Turner M.D. Moderation in all things is recognized as a major factor for a healthy and happy life. There is a strong and growing neoprohibition movement in America and the rights of moderate drinkers are in jeopardy. Gene Ford provides a well researched and scientifically documented expose of the prohibitionists and their historic roots in America. The health plan benefits of moderate drinking are thoroughly established along with the social benefits of preventing abuse. Responsible drinking alternatives are discussed and thoughtful plans for reaching moderate drinking public policy are outlined. This is an important book that provides modern answers to old questions about alcohol consumption, it's safety and moderation. Essential for everyone in the wine business. Extensive bibliography and index. Paperback, 320 pp. $19.95

HOW TO ORDER BY MAIL: Indicate the number of copies and titles you wish on the order form below and include your check, money order. or Master or Visa card number. California residents include 8.5% sale tax. There is a $5.00 S/H fee per order, regardless of how many books you order. (If no order form – any paper will do.)

ORDER FORM
WINE APPRECIATION GUILD
360 Swift Avenue So. San Francisco, CA 94080
Phone Toll Free: 800-231-WINE

Ship To: _____

Address: _____

City_____ State_____ Zip_____

Please send the following:

_____Copies	#501	Gourmet Wine Cooking The Easy Way	$12.95@_____
_____Copies	#502	New Adventures In Wine Cookery	$12.95@_____
_____Copies	#503	Favorite Recipes of California Winemakers	$9.95 @_____
_____Copies	#504	Dinner Menus With Wine	$9.95 @_____
_____Copies	#554	Wine Cellar Record Book	$32.50 @_____
_____Copies	#640	The Champagne Cookbook	$14.95 @_____
_____Copies	#641	Pocket Encyclopedia of California Wines	$14.95 @_____
_____Copies	#672	Wine In Everyday Cooking	$9.95 @_____
_____Copies	#673	California Wine Drink Book	$6.95 @_____
_____Copies	#727	Wine Lovers Cookbook	$12.95 @_____
_____Copies	#855	Pocket Encyclopedia of American Wines-East of the Rockies	$9.95 @_____
_____Copies	#914	Wine, Food And The Good Life	$9.95 @_____
_____Copies	#986	Fine Wine In Food	$9.95 @_____
_____Copies	#6508	Pocket Encyclopedia of American Wines-Northwest	$7.95 @_____
_____Copies	6509	The Benefits Of Moderate Drinking	$14.95 @_____

California residents 8.5% sales tax _____
Plus $5.00 shipping and handling (per order) _____

Please charge to my Master card or Visa card # _____

Expiration Date_____

Signature_____